SPEED VEGAN

by

ALAN ROETTINGER

Book Publishing Company, Summertown, Tennessee

Published by Book Publishing Company
P.O. Box 99
Summertown, TN 38483
1-888-260-8458
www.bookpubco.com

Printed in Canada

ISBN 13: 978-1-57067-244-6

16 15 14 13 12 11 10   9 8 7 6 5 4 3 2 1

Library of Congress Cataloging-in-Publication Data

Roettinger, Alan, 1952-
  Speed vegan : quick, easy recipes with a gourmet twist / by Alan Roettinger.
    p. cm.
  Includes bibliographical references and index.
  ISBN 978-1-57067-244-6 (alk. paper) *4773* *1111* *0/12*
  1. Vegan cookery. I. Title.
  TX837.R742 2010
  641.5'636--dc22
                        2010003551

Books Alive is a member of Green Press Initiative. We chose to print this title on paper with postconsumer recycled content, processed without chlorine, which saved the following natural resources:

78 trees
2,172 lbs of solid waste
35,779 gallons of water
7,429 lbs of greenhouse gases
25 million BTU

For more information, visit <www.greenpressinitiative.org>.

Savings calculations from the Environmental Defense Paper Calculator on the web at <www.edf.org/papercalculator>.

Back cover: Hot Eggplant and Seitan Open-Face Sandwich, 54–55; Campari-Braised Radicchio Salad with Grapefruit, 108–109

Front flap (clockwise from top left): Greta's Cannellini Salad with Mint, 71; Cucumbers with Pomegranate Vinaigrette, 72–73; Cool-and-Spicy Salad, 75; Blanched Bean Sprout Salad, 73

Back flap: Beet and Celery Root Salad, 68–69

You take from a recipe, but you give to a dish.

–Alan Roettinger

CONTENTS

ACKNOWLEDGMENTS

I AM ONE UNBELIEVABLY LUCKY GUY. Wonderful things just keep happening to me. Even sorrows and disappointments have somehow turned out for the best. Maybe lucky is the wrong word. Whenever I take the time to look, regardless of success or failure, I invariably see *kindness* within it all, a sweetness far too deliberate and consistent to be random. I feel the presence of that indefinable supreme existence, vibrating within me, looking out for me, and I know I'm beholden to it for everything. Don't ask me how, but sensing this presence fills me with both joy and gratitude—which is all it seems to want of me, and that works out quite well. I don't get the feeling it cares one bit about being acknowledged in books, but I care, so there you have it.

There are also some people I'm grateful for—special people who make my efforts worthwhile—and I want to acknowledge them too:

My profoundly beautiful wife, Marcia, an endless source of delight for me, without whose fierceness I might never have gotten my act together. Behind every great man there is a woman wishing he made more money. Private joke.

My son, Morgan, a treasure I never could have imagined, who manages to convey his love and admiration while simultaneously confronting my every weakness with piercing wit. He's been practicing reverse psychology since he was two years old.

I try to be my best self in large part for them—for what they mean to me, and what I feel they deserve.

I'm also grateful for the family of fine human beings at Book Publishing Company, who not only believed in me enough to take me on a second time but also have welcomed me into their extraordinary tribe with warmth and friendship. Special thanks to Bob and Cynthia Holzapfel, Warren and Barbara Jefferson, Barb Bloomfield (and Neal), Thomas Hupp, Rick Diamond, and Anna Pope. Heartfelt thanks to each of them for the unique talents and support they contributed to make this book possible—and fun!

Finally, I want to acknowledge and thank Jo Stepaniak, who not only fixed every one of my syntactical errors and made me look good, but did so in the most polite and respectful manner—teaching me how to write better without taking any credit. Although we've only met in writing, I consider her an invaluable and dear friend.

S P E E D
V E G A N

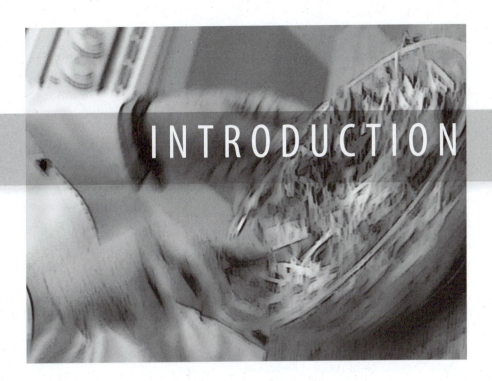

INTRODUCTION

WRITING THIS COOKBOOK presented a unique challenge on two fronts. As the title suggests, the primary feature of the recipes was to be speed, specifically the speed at which a home cook will be able to complete my recipes. This stretched the envelope for me. As a chef, I'm well familiar with the urgency to have everything ready on time. But the way I've dealt with this is to plan well and start early, not try to think inside a thirty-minute box! Compounding this, I also have a near-lifelong habit of taking whatever amount of time is needed to "do it right."

This is not meant to imply that there is a right and a wrong way to cook (although there probably is). On the contrary, "doing it right" is about reaching for something ephemeral. It refers to a state of mind, an uncompromising approach that, one hopes, may lead to excellence. If you put fast food at one end of a spectrum, "doing it right" would be at the opposite extremity. It's about refusing to cut corners that devalue the product, searching far and wide for the best ingredients, taking care to cut precisely, and adjusting schedules and temperatures to allow a gentle development of the ideal textures and flavors. Most of all, it's about putting your heart into what you do.

Time is a major factor in all this, because although you can develop skills that enable you to work quickly, with economy of movement and efficiency of technique, you can't make natural processes happen faster. To meet this challenge, I had to make myself think like a time-pressured home cook and come up with dishes I could admire that could also be completed by the average person in a half hour or less. This was the hard part, because so many wonderful ideas end up taking longer to manifest in the kitchen than they do in the mind. Let's just say that not everything I dreamed up made the thirty-minute cut.

The other half of the title was a test also, stemming from the fact that I'm not a vegan—at least I wasn't when I started working on this book—which is actually a good thing. I don't mean good for me, or good for the planet, or good for animals—I mean good for this cookbook. Here's why:

My motive in cooking has always been to create something extraordinary, something that thrills and delights the palate. When I'm working within a set of guidelines—such as low fat, gluten free, or nondairy—I regard these parameters as challenges, never as any sort of goal. My objective is clear and consistent: to transform something I absolutely must have (food) into something I deeply appreciate (deliciously satisfying food). Part of that goal is to also ensure that the food is at least vaguely healthful, so it doesn't come back to haunt my pleasure with ugly consequences.

In all of my cooking, this primary goal remains constant. The only difference in these particular recipes is that they also happen to be vegan friendly. And of course, this makes it all good—for me, for you, for the planet, and everything that lives. If you're entertaining any nonvegans, this food will help win them over, because I've made everything in the book to please a nonvegan palate (mine).

News Flash: I must now interrupt this introduction for an important update, inserted after the book's completion but before going to press. Although I still consider myself an omnivore (meaning I *can* eat anything), I have begun eating a strict vegan diet. After only a few weeks, I can say unequivocally that my body is ecstatic with the change. I have more energy, I need less sleep, and in my athletic activities I feel *invincible!* I'd say that's a pretty solid endorsement of the vegan diet, wouldn't you agree? Okay, just wanted you to know that—now back to the present (*your* present, my past). Isn't life exciting? So many interesting plot twists.

Before we get started, I would like to offer a word or two of encouragement for those readers who might find it daunting to enter the kitchen at all, let alone undertake the awesome task of preparing extraordinary food in short order:

Don't be intimidated. It's not rocket science. Making something good to eat is the most ancient activity of civilized human beings. If illiterate people could do it with stone knives and clay pots, surely you will be able to do it with today's refined tools. A recipe is just a guideline, the blueprint of a dish's construction, so you can follow along and repeat what someone else did. Don't feel in any way obligated to copy my approach. If anything strikes you as odd or distasteful, change it or leave it out. If an ingredient proves difficult or impossible to find, carry on without it or replace it with something you think might be just as good. Before long, you'll be creating entirely new dishes of your own, and that's when the real fun starts.

Keep in mind this maxim of mine: You *take* from a recipe, but you *give* to a dish. What will make your food extraordinary is not the recipe, or even the ingredients—it's *you.* That, my friends, is the secret of my success.

ESSENTIAL KITCHEN EQUIPMENT

DON'T FEEL DEFICIENT OR DELINQUENT if you lack any of the kitchen equipment mentioned in this book. You wouldn't believe how ill equipped most people's kitchens are, even very wealthy people's kitchens. During my time as a private chef, I've often walked into elegant, beautiful, designer kitchens tricked out with restaurant-style stoves, commercial refrigerators, gorgeous granite countertops, and little or no useful equipment! I'm not blaming these people—they never cook, so why would they even know what's missing? Of course, I've also encountered the other extreme, which is every drawer jammed with odd gadgets like hand-crank apple peelers, corn strippers, avocado slicers, asparagus steamers, and fractured remains of unidentifiable mechanisms that no one seems to dare throw away.

Why don't we just start fresh and keep it simple. I've broken it down into three lists: things you must have, things you will have a very hard time working without, and things that will make working a lot more fun. Some items you may want to get more of than the recommended minimum (such as bowls, spatulas, and the like), which is fine. Personally, I don't think you can ever have too many bowls. Or spoons. Or spatulas. Or whisks.

Whatever you do, don't go out and buy a "complete knife set," least of all an expensive one. I'm not against quality knives by any means—quite the contrary. But the knife set is not necessary, and you will not need all of the components (like the boning or filleting knives, if you're a vegan). You can do just about everything you need to do with two knives, listed in the first category. Let's get started.

MUST HAVE

APPLIANCE

Blender. Not counting a few industrial blenders, the Braun, with its triangular design, which encourages flow, and serrated blades, which retain their cutting prowess after long years of service, is the best blender I've ever used. The only trade-off is the speed control, which for some reason goes immediately into hyperdrive, even on the lowest setting. I still notice this single flaw every time I use it, but I've adjusted—which in itself is a testament to the effectiveness of the machine overall.

COOKWARE

Baking sheets. I use commercial sheet pans, which are heavier than the standard pans made for home use, because they conduct and hold heat much better and can double as broiling pans in a pinch. Unfortunately, these are made of aluminum, so it's important to line them with parchment paper when cooking or baking anything acidic (like tomatoes, for example) in order to prevent the aluminum from reacting with and contaminating the food. It's good to have at least one, but two would be better. I don't even know how many I have, and I use them all.

Saucepan, large. There are many uses for a large (2- to 3-quart) saucepan. Not only will it enable you to cook large quantities, but it will also facilitate some procedures involving smaller quantities. Although you may not fill it up with every use, you will find it easier to stir and move ingredients around during the initial steps if there is little or no crowding. It is important to have a proper lid for this pan, especially for cooking grains, when keeping moisture contained is essential. As for all cookware, a heavy bottom is very helpful for even heat distribution. All-Clad brand stainless steel pans with an aluminum core are the best (and most expensive—sorry!).

Saucepan, small. A fairly small (1- to $1^{1}/_{2}$-quart) saucepan is useful in a number of ways. It's ideal for making sauces, reheating one or two servings of soup or hot cereal, or making rice for up to four people. A tight-fitting lid will be essential for some feats.

Sauté pans. Although I know you will discover that having several sauté pans will help shorten the time it takes for you to make a complete meal, you can squeak by with one large pan (10 to 12 inches) and one small pan (6 to 8 inches). If they have lids, so much the better. I would avoid nonstick pans in general because you can get good results without them and the material used to make them is toxic—it inevitably gets into the food as well as the air you breathe. It's your life, though—your call.

Stockpot. A very large stockpot (with at least a 2-gallon capacity) is useful for making soups, but it's also essential for blanching vegetables and for cooking pasta. A lid will help water boil faster and keep the contents from boiling away too fast.

CUTLERY

Knife, large chef's. You will use a large chef's knife for most cutting and chopping tasks. To make your work as efficient and easy as possible, choose a knife with a blade at least 10 inches long. It may seem a bit daunting at first, but you'll find that having a long blade helps a lot, especially for chopping herbs. You might want to select a knife before looking at cutting boards. I use a 12-inch knife, so I also have a large cutting board to accommodate it. Next time I'm on TV, I'll show you how to use it, but until then, I recommend picking up a book or video that teaches basic kitchen techniques. That's how I learned—reading, watching, and doing.

Knife, small paring. A paring knife with a short blade is best, as it will give you better control for fine cutting and peeling. I suggest visiting a professional kitchen supply outlet, where you will find high-quality paring knives at near-disposable prices. My favorite (Swiss made!), by Victorinox (about $4), sports a red plastic handle that stands out among all the prep detritus and will help keep you from scraping it into the trash by mistake. It's the only knife I consider dishwasher safe.

TOOLS

Colander. Some tasks are near impossible to perform properly without some kind of colander. Having one will make many other tasks much easier. I highly recommend the kind that looks like a huge, reinforced coarse strainer (versus the classic bowl-with-holes kind). It allows for quick draining, it nests nicely in large bowls for storage, and, oddly enough, it cleans more easily than other kinds. Get the biggest one you can find.

Cutting board. I like a bamboo cutting board for beauty, but for practicality, I recommend one of those poly-plasticlike boards that resists stains and bacteria and can be put in the dishwasher. To protect your knife's edge, make sure to select a cutting board made of "self-healing" material, not hard plastic. Once you've invested in one all-purpose cutting board, you might want to get one or two smaller ones for quick work. It's also a good idea to use a separate cutting board for fruits, to keep their flavor from being tainted by residual garlic or onion juices that may be present, especially with wooden boards.

Grater. If you're choosing a single grater, you'll get the most uses out of a four-sided box grater, which has cutters of various sizes and shapes. Tip: Always wash the grater immediately after using it—this will save you a lot of scrubbing later on! Very often a rinse is all that's needed.

Hot pads. I know it's common sense that you'll need a hot pad for each hand, but I don't want any of my beloved fans to find out the hard way, so get two! Of course, you can always use a folded towel as a hot pad, but be careful—there is a very real danger of burning your hand if the towel is even slightly damp. There are some very cool silicone hot pads available now that will keep your hands safe even when wet.

Mixing bowls, large. Although I own quite a few glass and ceramic mixing bowls, I inevitably reach for my stainless steel bowls first, as I prefer their light weight, durability, and even their sound. I recommend having at least two of these bowls, as large as you can fit in your sink to wash.

Mixing bowls, small. You can't have too many mixing bowls, but you should definitely have at least two (again, I recommend stainless steel), with a capacity of 1 to 2 quarts (perhaps one of each size).

Pepper mill. I'm not trying to be a food snob here. Freshly ground pepper has a dynamic flavor that dissipates within a fairly short period of time. The preground pepper available in stores has oxidized, turning whatever flavor remains into an altogether different and utterly undesirable seasoning. Some health experts claim that whereas freshly ground pepper has beneficial properties, oxidized pepper is mildly toxic. Choose an adjustable pepper mill—a few out there have only one setting, and occasionally you'll want to adjust the grind from coarse to fine.

Silicone spatula. Silicone is heat-resistant, so a spatula made from it allows you to use it for stirring hot food in a pan as well as for standard food preparation. To be economical, you can start with one flat spatula and then add one with a slight scoop shape later on. They're each useful in their own way.

Spoon, slotted. My favorite slotted spoon is a Chinese strainer—a wide, wire-mesh affair attached to a bamboo stick that allows instant draining when scooping things out of boiling water or hot oil. I also have a few stainless steel spoons with round or rectangular holes that work quite well, if not as efficiently or elegantly.

Spoons, stainless steel. It's important to have a couple of stainless steel spoons for scooping, stirring, and of course, serving.

Spoons, wooden. When it comes to stirring implements, as anyone who cooks frequently will tell you, the more the merrier. I recommend having at least two wooden spoons, one round-ended and one flat. Bamboo spoons are the only kind I've found that resist warping and the absorption of flavors. They even survive the rigors of repeated dishwasher abuse, which regular wooden spoons do not weather well at all.

Strainer. Eventually, you may decide to get at least three strainers (fine, medium, and coarse), but starting out, a medium-fine-mesh strainer, 5 to 6 inches in diameter at the open end, will accomplish most tasks adequately. Think of one that is just barely fine enough to catch raspberry seeds.

Whisk. A whisk is a miraculous device. I have quite a few, in different shapes and sizes for various uses. If you're just starting out, I recommend buying a medium-size whisk, which would extend approximately $6\frac{1}{2}$ inches from the handle. Sooner or later you'll find a need for other sizes and shapes, but I'll leave that shopping adventure to you.

HARD TIME WORKING WITHOUT

APPLIANCE

Food processor. I was sorely tempted to put this in the "must have" category, but I didn't want to scare anyone off. Besides, I worked without one for two months on a job in Portugal, and although it was challenging, I survived. A food processor does not replace a knife—it has no subtlety or craft, and its blades only cut one way—but it makes quick work of some chores that otherwise are pure drudgery. It also does many things better than a blender, as it allows for fine chopping and even puréeing with a minimum of added liquid to keep the food moving. I have two: one with a 6-cup capacity for most jobs and a 2-cup "mini prep" for occasional small-quantity work.

COOKWARE

Stovetop grill. There are a few good versions of the stovetop grill, which is a thick, cast-iron sheet with ridges that you heat directly over the burner on your stove. It even leaves grill marks, just like the real thing. (I guess it kinda *is* the real thing, in its own way.) Of course, you can always use a regular outdoor grill, but for quick work, this is really easy and helpful (and it can be used year-round, in all types of weather).

TOOLS

Garlic press. There are few kitchen items more handy or more frequently used than a garlic press. The alternative is to mash and chop garlic by hand, which takes about ten times longer (I know because this is another tool that wasn't available in Portugal). I don't often endorse or recommend any particular brand of equipment, but the Zyliss (Swiss made) is the only one that really works right. The holes are the ideal size, and it doesn't break during the first year, like most of the other ones, whose names I won't mention. In fact, I've had the same one for twenty-five years and it's still working perfectly (again I say, Swiss made). Since it's made of aluminum, be careful to wash it often if you're pressing a lot of garlic. Otherwise, the aluminum will begin to react and bleed into the pressed garlic (you'll see it turning gray). Another point—very important—don't ever put it in the dishwasher! Even one pass will corrode it beyond repair. Same goes for anything else made of aluminum.

Measuring cups and spoons. To be honest, I almost never use measuring cups and spoons unless I'm baking or writing cookbooks, but since I've provided exact measurements, you'll have a hard time following the recipes unless you have measuring tools. On the other hand, this should serve as a between-the-lines hint that you really don't need to worry too much about measuring exactly. I suggest that you become familiar with what quantities look like, so you can become comfortable eyeballing amounts and freewheeling it in the kitchen. You'll have a lot more fun that way.

Parchment paper. When I was a pastry chef, I used to order commercial parchment sheets by the ream, but that's gross overkill for the home kitchen. So now I just go to the baking department of supermarkets and ask them for a few sheets. They usually just hand me about twenty-five of them, but even when they charge me, it comes to about a buck. These will be full-sheet size, which is roughly twice the size of a baking sheet you'd have at home, so cut them in half and you'll have enough to last you months. If the freeloading approach creeps you out, you can also buy parchment paper in many supermarkets as well as kitchen supply stores. However, most often it comes in a roll, which I find exasperatingly difficult to use because as soon as a piece is torn off, it insists on curling back up. Your call.

Salad spinner. I consider salad a minimum daily requirement, so for me it would be a genuine hardship to live without a salad spinner. It's a *Speed Vegan's* natural friend. It's fun to use, it makes lightning-quick work of whipping the water off lettuce, and it doubles as a bowl in which to soak and rinse the lettuce, and that can be especially helpful if you don't have a lot of big bowls. Don't get the kind with a hole in the bottom, or the only place you'll be able to use it is over the sink. (I don't know who the hell thought *that* was a good idea.)

Tongs. There is nothing more effective than a set of tongs for picking up hot foods (like baked potatoes or grilled vegetables) or for tossing salads without using your bare hands (especially useful if people are watching).

MAKES WORK MORE FUN IF YOU HAVE

Ceramic ginger grater. A ginger grater is what you use for grating fresh ginger, of course. The Japanese make beautiful ceramic graters that add an ethno-aesthetic design accent for your kitchen, too. I have one in the shape of a flounder, with both eyes looking up at me and an upturned tail for a handle. I keep the ginger on it, waiting for the moment to arise. Looks cool, works great.

Microplane grater. A relatively new culinary tool, the microplane grater was invented by a carpenter who suddenly realized that one of his razor-sharp precision tools would be ideal for grating the zest off a lemon in perfect, thin strips. I used to use the side of the grater that looks like someone poked it all over with a nail. Although that method still works, a microplane grater is a hundred times more fun and a whole lot safer, even considering how sharp the mini-blades are—I've lost count of the times I abraded my knuckles on the old nail-hole kind. It's ideal not only for grating citrus zest but also for making tiny curls and flakes of chocolate. Just don't try it on nutmeg or you'll cut yourself for sure!

More baking sheets, spatulas, and whisks. I know I've said it before, but it bears repeating: you can never have too many good tools! Get as many baking sheets, spatulas, and whisks as your personal tastes (and pocketbook) dictate.

Mortar and pestle. There's something incredibly satisfying about using a kitchen tool that has remained virtually unchanged since before recorded history. Get yourself a large, heavy-duty, seriously ethnic-looking mortar and pestle. I have several, but my favorite is a Thai stone mortar with a pestle made from coconut palm wood that makes a sound like some Neolithic musical instrument.

Pastry brush. I recommend buying an inexpensive, dishwasher-safe, silicone pastry brush, available at many supermarkets and kitchen supply stores. The natural-bristle brushes don't last, and they shed; plus they're made from some kind of animal hair anyway, so there you go. A pastry brush is very useful for dabbing vegetables with oil prior to grilling or for spreading Garlic Oil (page 38) on toast (mmm!).

Serrated knife. Once you've acquired a large chef's knife and a small paring knife (and recovered financially), a serrated knife is a good investment. It excels at cutting bread, very ripe tomatoes, and anything that tends to smush when you press down on it (even lightly) with a regular knife. Its sawing action can also make easier work of some odd jobs, like cutting the spiny skin off a pineapple or slicing watermelon.

Spice mill. A spice mill is really just a coffee grinder that is dedicated strictly for grinding spices. I've hand-pounded curry powder mixtures in a mortar, which is definitely fun, but a spice mill gets the job done in a tenth of the time (and without the blisters). Trust me, there is no comparison between freshly ground spices and jars of the same stuff preground, and you're more likely to take this extra step if you make it easy on yourself.

Superfine strainer. There will be times when you'll need to strain the fine bits out of a soup or sauce that a medium-mesh strainer won't catch. Don't let anyone sell you a chinois, by the way; it is much finer than you'll probably ever need in your life and very expensive. Someday you may want to get one for the fun of it, but it takes some time to use (and clean!), so it's hardly a *Speed Vegan* item. Just get a regular fine-mesh strainer.

STOCKING THE VEGAN PANTRY

THE ABILITY TO WHIP UP SOMETHING FABULOUS in a half hour or less is not innate; it must be acquired, in very much the same way as the ability to create something spectacular over several hours is acquired. There are a few basic skills that definitely help, such as holding a knife effectively and cutting ingredients accurately, and I highly recommend spending some time acquiring and developing these skills. However, in the short term we can do a lot to enable good results just by stocking our pantry with two categories of ingredients that I call essentials and acceptable shortcuts. The latter refers to commercially prepared foods, which represent a minor trade-off or ones that are well worth the compromise. It would be nearly if not completely impossible to make some things in less than thirty minutes without these items.

The modern pantry has three areas for storing ingredients, depending on whether the items are shelf stable, refrigerated, or frozen. Not all ingredients are acceptable shortcuts when stored in these various ways. For example, canned beans are by and large acceptable, but canned peas are an utter abomination. Dried thyme and dried oregano retain a lot of their aroma and taste, so they are fairly good substitutes for fresh thyme and oregano; dried cilantro and dried chives lose nearly all their flavor when dried, rendering them functionally useless.

I've taken the guesswork out of all this by dividing my pantry-stocking recommendations into these three groups. Note that some items that you may have previously considered shelf stable appear here in a different category. Nuts, for example, which contain fragile fats, will keep better and retain both their healthful qualities and optimum flavor when refrigerated for the short term and stored in the freezer for longer periods.

I've included a few recipes for homemade pantry items that will greatly enhance your *Speed Vegan* efforts. I have also indicated the best storage methods for each of them. All of these recipes adhere to the thirty-minutes-or-less rubric, and most of them can be done in five.

I haven't given quantities for the pantry items because it's up to the individual to determine how often a given ingredient will be used and in what amount. I do recommend, however, that you stock up on hard-to-find items such as ancho and pasilla chile powder, porcini powder, ras el hanout, saffron, and smoked paprika whenever you're in a store that carries them. If you're ordering online, it makes sense to buy as many items as you can afford at one time because the shipping cost will be comparatively less than when you order items individually. All of these ingredients will keep for a while, and having them on hand will greatly increase your chances of turning out something truly special.

Don't feel like you have to run out and buy all these items at once. In fact, I would advise against buying anything until you need it, because the longer you wait, the longer that item will remain fresh. Just let your pantry build up naturally as you go. If you're going to buy several items at once to save shipping costs, consider storing the ones you have no immediate plans for in the freezer until the need arises. Once you collect at least some quantity of the items on the list that follows, you'll be able to make anything in this book on short notice; you will only need to buy some fresh vegetables that day.

A final note: Always choose organic products whenever possible. Why? Because they don't have poisons on them or in them, that's why. And they taste better. And if you have a way to make sure they're grown locally, you'll get an added triple benefit: you'll have vastly fresher produce, you'll reduce your carbon footprint, and you'll be supporting your local community. Add it up: that's a win-win-win-win-win situation.

SHELF-STABLE INGREDIENTS

Shelf-stable items are those that do not require refrigeration, even after opening. However, it's still best to store them in a cool, dry, and dark area, especially away from direct sun. If you live in an area prone to natural disasters, like earthquakes or hurricanes, shelf-stable items are good to stock up on because they don't spoil (although bugs and rodents may be attracted to them for the same reason, so be aware of that). There are a few items called for in the recipes that are rather standard and easy to find, like cinnamon, cloves, thyme, and oregano, so I haven't listed them here. However, some of the ingredients in the following list may not be familiar to you or may take some hunting around to locate, or perhaps I just have something particular to say about them.

DRIED HERBS AND SPICES

Ancho chile powder. Ancho chile is a ripened (red), dried Mexican poblano pepper (the fresh, green form is the pepper used for *chiles rellenos*). The flavor is exotic and quite strong, enough to alter the character of a dish dramatically. Although ancho chiles are typically sold whole, many Mexican markets and specialty stores also carry them ground. If you can't find the powder, you can make your own by breaking up whole dried chiles (remove the stems first) and grinding them in a spice mill. You can control the amount of heat in the powder by removing all or most of the seeds.

Bay leaves. A single bay leaf has a way of infusing an entire dish with its delectable flavor and aroma, but that's only if it's a high-quality, fragrant bay leaf. Before you buy, give it the sniff test; it should emit an undeniably appealing aroma. A lot of what's out there is pretty sad. I've found Spice Islands California bay laurel to be fairly reliable, but the best ever were from The Spice House (see Online Shopping Sources, page 169).

Black peppercorns. It's important to always grind pepper fresh, at the time of use. This is true of any spice, because once you grind it, you expose a much greater surface area to the air, accelerating oxidation exponentially. You lose a lot of flavor that way, but you also lose nutritional as well as therapeutic value. Many spices have ancient medicinal applications, such as those used in the Ayurvedic system of healing and health, and it's best to retain as much of their inherent qualities as possible.

Cardamom seeds. I love cardamom and have been accused of overusing it, both in appropriate applications and unorthodox ones. With rare exceptions, I've vehemently disagreed with my critics because, well, love is love and follows its own logic. Cardamom is sold in green pods as well as decorticated, or removed from the pod. For the most part, I prefer buying seeds in whole pods because the pod protects the aromatics in the seed better, although even the decorticated seeds are a million times preferable to preground cardamom. Just so you know, I'm referring to green cardamom. There is also a black cardamom, used whole to flavor Indian dishes, but the latter are slow-cooked, sophisticated items, so there is really no *Speed Vegan* application for it that I know of.

Curry powder. There are curry powders and then there are curry powders. The mixture itself is a bit of blasphemy, as it purports to standardize something authentically Indian, whereas in Indian cuisine each cook builds the combination of spices needed for a particular dish on the spot, blending and adding as needed to achieve the right balance. Moreover, Indian cuisine varies greatly from region to region; North Indian food differs dramatically in character from the food of South India. However, for the Western cook with no knowledge of Indian cooking but an appreciation for its flavors, a lot can be accomplished with a good curry powder. I suggest trying different ones and selecting the most appropriate one for each particular application. The Spice House (see Online Shopping Sources, page 169) offers a fine selection of very different curry powders.

Garam masala. In Indian cuisine, garam masala (roughly, "hot spice mixture"), is a blend of pungent aromatics, ground together and used to enliven dishes with a vibrant note. The exact mixture varies from home to home and can contain any combination of bay leaves, black or green cardamom, cinnamon, cloves, coriander seeds, cumin, black cumin, nutmeg, mace, black or white peppercorns, or star anise (did I leave anything out?). The "heat" implied by the name refers to the pungent qualities of the spice mixture, not the stinging heat of chiles. Again, as with curry powder, this can be a useful ingredient for producing exotic flavors in *Speed Vegan* cookery. Look for commercially prepared garam masala at Indian grocery stores or specialty stores, or purchase it online at The Spice House.

Herbes de Provence. The signature flavors of Provence, France—basil, fennel, lavender, marjoram, rosemary, tarragon, and thyme—come together in a single blend of herbs called (appropriately enough) herbes de Provence, which is widely available in supermarkets.

Mixed peppercorns. More than the sum of its parts, mixed peppercorns (also called *quatre épices*), a combination of black, green, pink, and white peppercorns, can be found in most well-stocked markets and specialty stores. Freshly ground, this mixture creates a complex seasoning, with flavor notes you won't get from any of the different peppercorns individually. Pink and green peppercorns are particularly fragrant, each providing a unique, exotic twist.

Pasilla chile powder. Like the ancho, the pasilla is a dried chile with a distinctive flavor. The powder can be very hard to find, so don't kill yourself trying—just keep an eye out for it in Hispanic food markets. It keeps for long periods in an airtight container. If you are able to locate dried pasilla chiles whole, you can grind them in the same way as the anchos. Not to complicate things for you, but some shopkeepers don't know the difference and will sometimes sell ancho chiles under the name pasilla. I'm probably being charitable;

they may know exactly what they're doing, but I'd rather err on the side of charity.

Ras el hanout. A Moroccan spice mixture, available at Mediterranean or Arabic markets and at specialty stores, ras el hanout has a character similar in some ways to curry powder, imparting a complex, very fragrant, uniquely North African flavor. "Ras el hanout" means "top of the shop" in Arabic, indicating the shopkeeper's signature blend. In Morocco, the specific mixture varies from shop to shop and may contain well over twenty ingredients, including some unexpected ones like cassia bark, lavender, orris root, rosebuds, or even hashish, depending on the shopkeeper's expertise and predilection. Outside Morocco, most ras el hanout is commercially produced in France (sans the hashish) and is fairly standardized. My favorite comes from The Spice House in Chicago (see Online Shopping Sources, page 169) and includes whole saffron threads.

Red chile powder. Indian grocery stores carry a very hot and fragrant red chile powder, but cayenne is a good substitute.

Saffron threads. The saying "a little goes a long way" truly applies to saffron. A mere pinch will hurl a whole potful of whatever you're cooking into exotic terrains. Once the province of kings (it was worth more than its weight in gold), saffron comes from a purple crocus that yields only three threads (stigma) per flower. Saffron is now much more affordable, in part because it is cultivated in Spain as well as in Kashmir.

Sea salt. I keep both coarse and fine Celtic salt on hand for the best flavor and mineral content. A lot of people think that salt is just something to bring out the flavor of food—and it will—but good salt is much more than that. Hand-harvested salt from the ocean is full of trace minerals and has a delicious flavor of its own that it will impart to the food. My favorite is actually not harvested from the sea, but it is the oldest sea salt on earth: Himalayan pink salt, formed millions of years ago, when the seas had not yet been polluted, as the world's highest peaks were pushed up from the ocean floor. Cool, huh?

Smoked salt. I use smoked salt rarely, but it keeps indefinitely and is ideal for adding a smoky flavor to dishes that warrant it (see "Smoked" Portobello Mushroom Salad, page 103).

Spanish smoked paprika. Once a rare and hard-to-find item, Spanish smoked paprika is now fairly easy to find (if you're looking for it). Like saffron, a small quantity of smoked paprika can go a long way in turning an ordinary dish in an extraordinary direction.

FATS

Extra-virgin coconut oil. If you're going to fry something, extra-virgin coconut oil is the best vegan medium for it. It's a highly saturated fat and remains quite firm at room temperature (unless your room is somewhere near the equator). It has a strong but pleasant coconut flavor, which limits its application to dishes that go well with it, such as Southeast Asian, South Indian, Central and South American, and sub-Saharan (not sounding so limited now, huh?).

Extra-virgin red palm oil. Red palm oil is used extensively in Brazilian cooking, and now a high-quality extra-virgin form of it is available in the United States at natural food stores. Don't confuse this with refined dende oil, the standard form of red palm oil used in Brazil, which I think may be better suited to lubricating engine parts.

FLAVORINGS, SWEETENERS, AND SUCH

Agave nectar. About twice as sweet as sugar, agave nectar is made from agave juice (which is also used to make tequila) and is now widely used, especially by vegans, as an alternative to honey. I was disappointed to learn recently that, despite the advertising, agave nectar is a far cry from the *agua miel* (fresh agave juice) I grew up with in Mexico. I had thought agave nectar was merely a filtered, possibly flash-pasteurized version. As it turns out, the processing not only destroys enzymes and removes minerals but also yields a highly refined product virtually identical to high-fructose corn syrup. Oh well. There isn't a whole lot of it used in this book, and it may still seem better than ripping off the bees in your estimation.

Chinese salted black beans. Available at Asian and specialty markets, Chinese salted black beans are black beans that have been fermented, salted, and dried. A mere teaspoonful will add tremendous depth of flavor to sauces and dressings.

Dark chocolate. Remember that chocolate is good for you, but only dark chocolate, preferably with a minimum of 70 percent cacao solids. Did you know that a recent study in Sweden showed that heart attack survivors who ate dark chocolate at least twice a week afterward cut their risk of dying from heart disease by 300 percent over those poor fools who wouldn't eat it? They don't call it *theobroma* (food of the gods) for nothing. I eat it pretty much every day, and not just for the heart that pumps blood.

Dried wild mushrooms. The wild mushrooms I use most often are chanterelles, morels, porcinis, and shiitakes. Each variety has distinctive qualities, not only in flavor and aroma but also in texture and appearance. Drying concentrates the flavor, which comes out with a vengeance when the mushrooms are reconstituted (this is a good thing). Because dried wild mushrooms can be quite expensive, you may prefer to wait until the need arises before investing in them. I like to keep at least some shiitakes around because they go well with a lot of last-minute dishes. Morels are my absolute favorite, but I almost never can keep any in stock because I use them up as soon as I get them.

Dulse. Rich in minerals, with a pleasant purply color, a delicious, mildly briny taste, and melt-in-your-mouth texture, dulse is an ideal "introductory" sea vegetable for people who balk at the idea of eating seaweed. It's delicious in salads and soups or just out of your hand as a salty snack. Look for it at natural food stores in the macrobiotic section.

Mirin. Also known as sweet sake, mirin provides the distinctive flavor in teriyaki sauce. It is a rice wine similar to sake but sweeter and with a lower alcohol content. It adds a uniquely Japanese touch to sauces and condiments.

Palm sugar. A delectable alternative to brown sugar, palm sugar is harvested from coconut palms in Southeast Asia. It is available granulated and as a paste. Indian *gur*, or *jaggery*, made from sugarcane, is a decent substitute.

Pomegranate molasses. A Middle Eastern staple made by reducing pure pomegranate juice to a thick syrup, pomegranate molasses imparts a pleasant, tangy fruit note. I like using it with dishes that are not Middle Eastern in origin, just to stretch the envelope a little. Sometimes it doesn't really work, but it's always worth a try. Many supermarkets now carry it in their international sections.

Porcini mushroom powder. Porcini mushroom powder is simply ground porcini mushrooms. You can grind them yourself in a spice mill. You can also make a wild mushroom powder with a combination of wild mushrooms. I've done this when I've had a few stray dried mushrooms of different types but not enough to make a mushroom dish of any consequence. A mere teaspoon of the powder will influence bland dishes (like tofu) gorgeously.

Tamarind concentrate. Tamarind is a sour, pulpy seed pod that grows in tropical and subtropical climates. In Mexico, it's used to make a refreshing cold drink called *agua de tamarindo.* In Southeast Asia and India, it's used in cooking not only to add a sour element but also, specifically, for its unique, characteristic flavor. Removing the pulp from the pod and separating it from the seeds is laborious, but commercially prepared tamarind concentrate (also called tamarind paste) takes the headache out of the equation and makes this delicious ingredient readily available to the home cook in any country.

Tekka. I'm not sure how this macrobiotic condiment came to be invented, but tekka is a terrific addition to the macrobiotic-food-lover's larder. It's a kind of moist powder made from burdock root, lotus root, carrot, sesame, and hatcho miso, cooked very slowly, yielding a dark, potent flavor. In addition to the recipe in this book (Lotus Root Soba with Tekka, page 113), there are several informal uses for tekka, such as sprinkling it over steamed vegetables or brown rice. Look for it at natural food stores in the macrobiotic section.

Vanilla extract. Don't waste money on the cheap, flavorless stuff! Look for Tahitian vanilla or, at the very least, Madagascar bourbon vanilla. The cost is higher but the flavor is well worth it. When I was a pastry chef at a billionaires' country club, I once had an argument with a cheapskate purchasing guy about this. To settle it, I poured a teaspoon of good Tahitian vanilla into one shot glass and the hideous stuff he had ordered into another. I let him "shoot" the good stuff first, suggesting he might get a hint of the exotic orchid plant the vanilla pod comes from. It brought an involuntary smile to his parsimonious lips. Then I had him shoot the other. He actually spat, and that was that. As I recall, there's a saying about catching more flies with honey than vinegar. Not a vegan saying, of course.

Vegetable bouillon cubes. One excellent way to add a mega splash of flavor to a soup, a sauce, or any juicy dish is to drop in a cube or two of vegetable bouillon. I threw one into mashed potatoes once, with striking results. I use it for pumping up rice or couscous too.

PASTA AND GRAINS

Basmati rice. Make sure you buy true basmati! Look for it at an Indian grocery store, if possible, because most so-called basmati rice in other stores is not genuine. Ask for Dehraduni basmati. This is not just a starch to bulk up your meal; this is a delicious partner to virtually any vegetable dish, especially those with a juicy sauce. Unlike polished white rice, basmati is hand processed and retains a little of the bran (look at it with a magnifying glass and you'll see). The grains fluff lengthwise into elegant, long, fragrant gems. The smell of true basmati cooking is downright intoxicating. Once you've had the real thing, impostors will be obvious to you on sight (and smell).

Brown rice pasta. This product is the closest to durum wheat (regular white) pasta that I've tried. Unlike other alternatives, it holds together well and retains a good *al dente* texture.

Buckwheat soba noodles. Wheat-sensitive people should check the ingredients because very often buckwheat soba noodles (as well as lotus root soba noodles and mugwort soba noodles) contain some wheat flour. Macrobiotic products are usually 100 percent buckwheat.

Since I began working on this book, I discovered that precooked fresh buckwheat soba noodles are now available in vacuum-sealed packages at many natural food stores as well as at Asian markets. Precooked fresh soba noodles are not only speedy to cook (they need just a brief warming in hot water), but they also have a texture that is far superior to the dried ones. You can use the precooked fresh soba noodles in place of the dried form in any of the recipes that call for soba noodles.

Farro pasta. An ancient relative of wheat, farro is grown in northern Italy. Although whole-grain farro pasta can be hard to find, it is far superior to whole wheat pasta both in flavor and texture. It is not exactly gluten free, but wheat-sensitive people can usually enjoy it without a problem. The whole grain itself has a texture that is a cross between wheat berries and barley, with a delicious flavor unlike either. Alas, it takes far too long to cook for the recipes in this book. However, if you're ordering farro pasta, I recommend adding a small bag of whole farro berries to your order so you can try it in its unprocessed form at least once.

Papadums. Sold primarily at Indian grocery stores, papadums (also called papads) are dried wafers made from spiced lentil paste that puff into unusually light, crisp, utterly delicious crackers when fried or toasted over a flame. If you've ever been to an Indian restaurant, you know what I'm talking about.

Quinoa. An ancient grain originally grown in the Andes mountains of Peru, quinoa is now grown organically in the United States and is widely available in natural food stores and some supermarkets. It's a whole protein, highly digestible, with a distinctive texture and flavor.

Red quinoa. A close cousin of regular quinoa, red quinoa is a bit firmer in texture, with a richer taste and a dark rust color. Not as easy to find, but gaining ground slowly.

Saifun (mung bean threads). Saifun are the glass noodles that appear in Asian dishes. Unlike other noodles, saifun are made from mung beans, which are a legume, not a grain.

VINEGARS

Balsamic vinegar. Pretty well known by now, balsamic vinegar is a fairly recent addition to the American food scene, but it has been treasured in Italy since the Middle Ages. But that's not even half the story. What we casually pick up in half-liter bottles at our supermarkets is not true balsamic vinegar but an imitative (albeit very tasty) commercial product that tastes vaguely like the real thing. Real balsamic vinegar is a labor of love, involving as much craft, tradition, and certification as the finest brandy. It can cost up to $400 for a 100-milliliter bottle, and it is typically doled out in drops and drams, not whisked gratuitously into salad dressings. But don't worry, that kind is not an ingredient in any of the recipes in this book. I just thought you'd like to know the roots.

Brown rice vinegar. Made from fermented brown rice, brown rice vinegar is mild, making it ideal for subtle salad dressings or any dishes that include traditional Japanese flavors, such as shiitake mushrooms, ginger, shiso, or tamari. I prefer brown rice vinegar hands down over the more mainstream "rice vinegar" found in supermarkets. It has a better flavor, and most brands are organic.

Red wine vinegar. Some dishes simply must have red wine vinegar. Greek salad wouldn't be the same with any other vinegar. When I add a little splash of vinegar to something for added dimension (like *peperonata*, an Italian roasted pepper dish), I almost always choose red wine vinegar.

Sherry vinegar. Real Spanish sherry vinegar has a complex, rich background of flavor. Like its Italian cousin, balsamic vinegar, sherry vinegar is aged and has specific certification requirements. Far from merely sour, sherry vinegar is like a poem, with nuances and delectable subtleties.

White balsamic vinegar. Balsamic vinegar (see above) is characterized by its slightly sweet mildness. This is a valuable feature for "lipophobes," who wrongly believe all fats are inimical to their health, because you can use balsamic vinegar to make a nicely balanced salad dressing with less oil. Little do they know, you can accomplish the same results by adding some sugar to any vinegar, which is basically what commercial producers use to make balsamic vinegar less tart. White balsamic vinegar has the same mild nature, with a bright, fresh character and none of the heaviness and dark color of regular balsamic (that's "regular" as opposed to "traditional" balsamic—again, see above). I use it when I want that mild, bright quality without the dark color.

White wine vinegar. Like white balsamic and rice vinegar, white wine vinegar is the milder sister of the full-bodied vinegars. It makes an ideal pairing with herbs like chervil, chives, lavender, or tarragon that would be bowled over by the gutsier red wine vinegar.

UNREFRIGERATED, *BUT...*

Some fresh produce fares better at room temperature than when refrigerated. Tomatoes, a good example, lose their wonderful fresh tomato flavor when they are refrigerated. However, fruits and vegetables spoil much faster at room temperature, and especially in a warm room. So keep the following out, but keep an eye on them:

- fresh ginger
- lemons
- limes
- onions
- potatoes (store in a dark place)
- shallots
- tomatoes

REFRIGERATE AFTER OPENING

Artichoke hearts. For the recipes in this book, use plain artichoke hearts packed in water (not marinated), preferably in glass jars. I recommend the small whole artichokes, as they are the most tender and flavorful. Some good artichokes can be found frozen; however, they are rather more expensive than those in jars. Supermarket frozen artichokes are reasonably priced, but I've found them to be tough and lacking in flavor.

Beans. There are only a few things I consider acceptable as canned food, and beans are among the top two or three. I keep a supply of black beans, garbanzo beans (also known as chickpeas), navy beans, pinto beans, and red beans. I also keep on hand cannellini beans (Italian white beans), which are similar to navy beans but are longer and much creamier, with a distinctive taste that lends itself particularly well to combining with Mediterranean flavors and textures.

Capers. I prefer the tiny nonpareils to the larger capers, but this is an aesthetic choice; the flavor is pretty much the same. You decide.

Chipotles en adobo. Recipe-ready Mexican chipotle chiles, reconstituted and prepared in a sauce, are known as *chipotles en adobo.* They can be served as a fiery condiment with a Mexican meal; blended with tomato, garlic, and onion to form the flavor base for spicy sauces; or chopped and added to soups, beans, and stews. They are quite spicy, so be sparing until you become familiar with them.

Coconut milk. Thai coconut milk is inexpensive and delicious. I keep a couple of cans in my pantry for sudden urges that come up in the middle of cooking anything with an Asian flavor.

Diced tomatoes. I like to keep a few containers of diced tomatoes on hand for a quick pasta sauce, to add to a vegetable soup, or to use in any number of dishes that need just a bit of tomato to round them out. I used to buy them in cans, but after reading about BPA, a toxic chemical in the lining of cans that reacts with the acid in tomatoes and leaches into them, I've switched to using only tomatoes in glass jars or aseptic cartons.

Hoisin sauce. There is some controversy in the health-freak community regarding commercially made hoisin sauce (perhaps it involves poor-quality ingredients, maybe MSG). You decide. On the other hand, you might want to try my recipe for a homemade version in my book *Omega-3 Cuisine.* Homemade is bound to be better because most commercial products have been made cheaper by cutting corners, both in flavor and health benefits. I like to keep hoisin on hand for building interesting layers of flavor in complex sauces. The tamarind in hoisin adds a pleasant tang to Asian hot-sour-pungent sauces.

Natto miso. Not easy to find, and not absolutely essential, but a good thing to have around, natto miso isn't like the regular miso you may be familiar with. It's actually more like a sweet chutney, made with ginger, sea vegetables, barley malt, and fermented whole barley. Look for it wherever macrobiotic food is sold.

Peanut butter. Yes, natural peanut butter (the kind that contains only peanuts and maybe salt) will survive a long time unrefrigerated, but the oils in it will degrade long before you can detect rancidity over the strong peanut taste. I recommend keeping all nuts, nut butters, and oils cold. Plus, storing natural peanut butter in the refrigerator will keep the oil from separating out.

Roasted red peppers. I've gotten a lot of practice, so it takes only a few minutes for me to roast and peel my own red peppers, but for most people it will save a lot of trouble to just buy a jar or two and keep them on hand. (Even I do this for extreme situations.) Just be sure to rinse them well before using, to get that "jar taste" off them, and remove the seeds and any burned skin the producers may have left on.

Roasted yellow peppers. It's a little harder to find roasted yellow peppers than the red ones, so if you run across any, my advice is to buy a couple of jars.

Sriracha sauce. A Vietnamese sweet-and-spicy red chile sauce, Sriracha is now a fairly ubiquitous table condiment in Asian restaurants. This is a very useful ingredient, even in Western-oriented dishes, for adding a stab of heat. Sugar has been used for a long time in Chinese cooking to coax the heat and flavor out of chiles, and Sriracha sauce does an excellent job of that.

Tahini. I used to buy only Middle Eastern tahini (sesame paste) for some food-snob reason I now can't recall, but since I value organically produced seed and nut butters, I go for American or European brands (depending on where I am, of course).

Thai green curry paste. Buyer beware! There are some vegan-friendly green curry pastes available, but traditional Thai versions include dried shrimp paste, so read the label.

Thai red curry paste. Thai red curry paste has the same issue as Thai green curry paste. Read the label!

Tofu, silken. If you're just stocking your pantry and don't have an immediate use for tofu, I recommend buying the unrefrigerated kind, packed in sealed aseptic cartons. It lasts longer and saves space in the refrigerator. However, the only kind packaged this way is silken tofu, a very smooth-textured tofu with a high moisture content that is not suitable for all applications. Its soft, creamy consistency (even in the extra-firm variety) makes it ideal for soups, such as Tuscan Kale and Coconut Soup with Tofu (page 65). Silken tofu is also best for blending into sauces, desserts, and anything that needs a smooth-textured result. Otherwise, fresh is always better (see the listing for fresh tofu in the Keep Refrigerated section, page 32).

Tomato purée. I prefer Italian *passata di pomodoro,* a minimally processed tomato purée, now widely available in glass jars rather than in cans. The beauty of reclosable jars is that you can use just a tablespoon or so to add tomato flavor to a dish and easily store the remaining purée for the next use.

White hominy. Called *nixtamal* in Mexico, hominy dates back to pre-Columbian times. Basically, it's white corn that has been dried and then cooked in limewater, a process that removes the germ and outer skin but improves the absorbability of amino acids and B vitamins (especially niacin) and boosts the calcium content. It also makes the corn more palatable and easier to digest. Hominy is what corn tortillas and tamales are made of, and although it's not a whole grain, it's highly nutritious and well worth the trade-off (in my humble opinion).

KEEP REFRIGERATED

Obviously, you won't be buying every single fresh ingredient called for in this book at once. If you did, your refrigerator would become an impenetrable jungle, and most of it would rot before you got around to using it. The purpose of this category is to list just a few things that are good to keep on hand, since they will come up often and they enhance many quick-and-easy dishes with a burst of fresh flavor. There are certainly others, but the following are ones I never like to be without.

Cilantro. Also known as coriander (the oddly lesser-known English word for it), cilantro is both loved and reviled (obviously, I put it in the loved category). The entire plant is flavorful—leaves, stems, and roots—although only the green parts are used in the recipes in this book. I've been accused of overusing cilantro (by Americans who are more accustomed to a bland gringo diet), but I stand firm in my liberal application of it.

Green chiles. Indian green chiles or Mexican serranos are ideal whenever green chiles are called for.

Mellow white miso. There are several varieties of miso (and I recommend trying them all), but mellow white miso is the most versatile because it combines well with other ingredients, adding a lightly salty, agreeably fermented (some would say cheesy) flavor. Miso is rich in live probiotics, so it's best to avoid cooking it, adding it instead after the cooking is done, as in miso soup.

Parsley. Italian flat-leaf parsley has the best flavor. It's much more than a garnish, bringing balance and fresh herb taste to European, Latin American, Mediterranean, Middle Eastern, and North African cuisines. It has been credited with counteracting the bad-breath effect of garlic, which is a major plus for garlic lovers like yours truly (and their lovers)!

Peeled garlic. Buying peeled garlic will save you a lot of time, and more often than not, it's in better shape than whole garlic. Unless you're good at judging freshness, a lot of times the whole garlic you'll get at supermarkets is old, dried out, or even rotten. At least in a jar you can see if it's fresh. If you stuff a paper towel into the jar to absorb excess moisture, the garlic will stay remarkably fresh for a week or longer in the refrigerator. I buy a huge container at a wholesale club and add more paper towels as I use the garlic, to keep the empty space filled. After about a week or two, I use the remaining garlic to make Roasted Garlic Purée (page 39), and then buy a new jar. This prevents the garlic from spoiling and keeps me supplied with both roasted and fresh garlic at all times.

Scallions. Always have at least one bunch of scallions on hand. Two is better, so when you use a bunch, you'll have one left while you run to the store.

Tofu, fresh. Whenever a recipe calls for tofu to be stir-fried, deep-fried, or treated in any other than a very gentle manner, I use extra-firm fresh tofu. Silken tofu is far to fragile to keep its shape in a dish like Tofu and Soba Noodles with Hot-Sweet-Sour-Pungent Sauce (page 122). Always store any unused portion of tofu in its original container in the refrigerator, with plenty of water to keep it moist.

REFRIGERATE, OR FREEZE FOR LONGER STORAGE

Almond oil. Sometimes I want a very mild (some would say neutral-tasting) oil that will present no competition to other ingredients with similarly subtle flavors. On these occasions, I use organic almond oil because it is the only such oil I know of that has not been refined (meaning stripped of nutritional content and attacked with caustic chemicals).

Extra-virgin olive oil. Unlike nut and seed oils, olive oil is pressed from the fruit, not the seed. So it's very important to get the first pressing, which is what "extra-virgin" means. After that, heat and even caustic chemicals may be used to get more oil out of the leftover mash, which then is subjected to a harsh refining treatment. With the exception of extra-virgin oils, all oils that are shelf stable have been refined by a process that includes exposure to toxic chemicals and high heat, which effectively strips out nutrients and leaves damaged molecules. Trust me, you don't want to eat any refined oil. Ever.

Flax oil. As I explained in my first cookbook, *Omega-3 Cuisine*, I highly recommend Udo's Choice 3-6-9 Oil Blends, which combine flax with other seed oils in a blend that provides both omega-3 and omega-6 fats in ideal proportions. I use Udo's DHA blend exclusively because it also includes a plant-based form of DHA, which is essential to the health and optimum functioning of the brain, eyes, heart, and nerve cells. But, of course, you can use whichever brand of flax oil you prefer.

Toasted sesame oil. Because of its strong toasted flavor, it's sometimes hard to tell if toasted sesame oil is fresh or has gone slightly rancid, which is a good reason to keep it refrigerated like the rest of the oils. I buy only Japanese toasted sesame oil because the Japanese invented it and (especially) because they have very high standards of quality and excellence.

Truffle-infused virgin olive oil. Although it is a luxury item, once you experience the flavor-enhancing power of truffle-infused virgin olive oil, you'll be hooked. Either that or you'll hate it, and that'll be one less thing you'll need to have clogging your refrigerator space.

Walnut oil. I use organic walnut oil on occasion for its mild, nutty flavor, which blends nicely with likewise mild vinegars and goes well with mild, tender lettuce. Never cook with it, as heat will turn its flavor bitter and destroy the antioxidant content.

FROZEN

It's always good to have a pack or two of corn and peas in the freezer, for ease as well as for emergencies. I keep frozen sliced shiitake mushrooms and sliced red, yellow, and green peppers (mixed) on hand, too. The freezer is also where I store nuts of all kinds to protect them from turning rancid (the nuts and seeds used in the recipes in this book include almonds, cashews, flaxseeds, hazelnuts, sesame seeds, and sunflower seeds). And I always have a jar of shaved dark chocolate curls in the freezer for use at the slightest whim. Here are a few other items you may want to have on hand for the recipes that follow.

Brown rice, cooked. Because it takes a minimum of forty-five minutes to cook, I suggest that whenever you make brown rice, make a lot of it and freeze the leftovers in batches of 2 or 4 cups each for use on a moment's notice. Cooking brown rice is very easy. Simply rinse the rice in a strainer, and then put it in a pot with $2\frac{1}{4}$ cups of water per cup of rice. Add a pinch or more of salt and bring to a boil. Stir once, cover, and turn the heat down to the lowest setting. Cook the rice, undisturbed, for 45 minutes. Remove the cover and fluff gently with a spoon or spatula. If any water remains, increase the heat to medium and cook until it has been absorbed. To freeze, first spread the rice out on a baking sheet to help it cool down quickly. Once the rice is cold, pack it in your preferred container. Pack it in as thin a layer as possible so it will thaw quickly. You may also prefer to skip the cooking part and buy frozen cooked brown rice at your favorite natural food store.

Cocoa powder. As with chocolate, buy the best quality you can find (and afford). After sampling a few, you will settle on one that tastes best to you. I've been stuck for years on Cacao Barry Extra Brute (fairly hard to find), but Valrhona is an excellent second choice. Signs of high quality include a reddish-brown color, a complex floral bouquet, and a pleasantly bitter taste (I know that sounds a bit oxymoronic, but high-quality cocoa barely needs sweetening, if at all). Call me a fanatic, but I keep cocoa in the freezer (sealed in an airtight container) because it contains fat (very delectable fat), and I want to protect it from turning rancid. Because cocoa has such a strong flavor, it may be difficult to detect rancidity until the cocoa just doesn't taste "right." Cocoa is the food of the gods; in my opinion, every precaution must be taken to preserve its subtle aromatics, bioflavonoids, and antioxidants.

Edamame. Unless you're planning to serve them in the pod, sushi-bar style, I recommend buying frozen shelled edamame. All they'll need is a light blanching, straight from the package, and they'll be ready to eat. (For you troglodytes who don't get out much, edamame are green soybeans.)

Green garbanzos. A relatively new product in the West, green garbanzos are well known in India, where they're sold dried and are generally cooked to death. Fresh green garbanzos, similar in character to Japanese edamame, are now available frozen. They need only a light blanching and can be eaten out of hand as a snack or tossed in salads, the same way edamame are used.

GETTING AHEAD

Last—but well above least—it's important to have a few basic home-made staples on hand that you can pull out and use to enhance a dish you're making, augment a meal, or jumpstart something to create "from-scratch" authenticity. Think of these as pre-recipe recipes.

The recipes that follow in the Jump Starts section may be unfamiliar, perhaps even a little unusual, but eventually you'll find them nearly indispensible—standard pantry items that support a *Speed Vegan* in the kitchen. Getting a salad done quickly on Monday night is enabled by taking a little time to make a batch of Balsamic Vinaigrette (page 44) on Saturday morning. Making a dressing or sauce will take less time (and will taste much better) if you've already got some Roasted Garlic Purée (page 39) or Sundried Tomato Paste (page 43) on hand. Come home, throw some potatoes in the oven, and go work out; come back, slice open the potatoes, pour in some Garlic Oil (page 38), and sprinkle with salt. Yum. You can literally have a baked potato and a great salad done in less than thirty minutes of active working time this way. Same thing for the morning, except with Brown Rice Cereal instead of potatoes—once you've done the prep, all you'll need to do is cook the cereal (with virtually no hands-on work).

Once you get the hang of it, you'll be able to pick out your favorite dressings, sauces, and condiments from the recipes in this book and add them to your must-have-on-hand pantry items. The recipes in the Jump Starts section are just a small selection to get you started.

JUMP STARTS

GARLIC OIL

Makes about 1 cup

Of all the basic pantry items I keep on hand, this is the one I need to replenish the most. It's so flavorful and versatile, it just seems to disappear. Fortunately, it takes mere minutes to prepare. I use an oil blend that supplies omega-3 and omega-6 fats in a 2:1 ratio, sometimes adding some olive oil for a more Mediterranean flavor. This recipe blends flax and olive oils, but you can use whichever combination suits your palate. You'll find dozens of uses for this preparation, trust me. Garlic Oil keeps for a week in the refrigerator, but to be honest, this has never been put to the test in my house. You'd be surprised how fast a cup of this will go. I often will simply add some more oil to the bottle when it gets low, sometimes pressing another clove of garlic or two into it as well, sometimes not. I go on taste. It's not rocket science, after all.

> 7 cloves peeled garlic
> ¼ teaspoon sea salt (optional)
> ½ cup flax oil
> ½ cup extra-virgin olive oil

Chop the garlic coarsely. Then pound it to a paste in a mortar with the salt, if using. Add a few tablespoons of the flax oil and mash the garlic and oil together. Add the remaining flax oil and olive oil and mix well. Pour into a jar or bottle, cover tightly, and refrigerate until ready to use.

That's the fun method. The quick method is to crush the garlic directly into the jar using a garlic press, and then add the salt, if using, and both of the oils. Cover tightly and shake vigorously. Refrigerate until ready to use.

Per tablespoon: calories: 122, protein: 0 g, fat: 13 g, carbohydrate: 0 g, fiber: 0 g, sodium: 0 mg, omega-3 fatty acids: 3.5 g

ROASTED GARLIC PURÉE

Makes about 2 cups

Chances are good that you won't be eating this by itself, but it's a wonder-ful flavor enrichment for soups, sauces, and salad dressings. In fact, you'll be surprised how fast a couple of cups will disappear. Like Garlic Oil (page 38), this is an excellent vampire repellent (go ahead, laugh—*I've* never been bitten). Unfortunately, this can also repel people, but I've found that including a good amount of fresh parsley in the same dish will significantly mitigate the dragon-breath effect. I'm told it's the chlorophyll that does the trick.

> 2 cups peeled garlic cloves
> 2 tablespoons extra-virgin olive oil
> ½ teaspoon sea salt
> ¼ teaspoon freshly ground black pepper

Preheat the oven to 375 degrees F.

Trim the root ends off the garlic cloves. Toss the garlic in a bowl with the olive oil, salt, and pepper.

Stack 10 sheets of heavy-duty aluminum foil on a work surface, rumpling them slightly so that they don't lie exactly flat. The idea behind this is to create some air pockets, which act as heat buffers to prevent the garlic from burning. Put a sheet of parchment paper on top of the foil. Pile the garlic mixture into a nice mound in the middle of the paper and fold the entire stack of paper and foil over it, folding and crimping the edges to form a tight seal.

Put the package in the oven and roast for about 1 hour, turning the oven down to 325 degrees F for the last 15 minutes. Remove the package from the oven and allow it to cool completely.

Open the package and slip the roasted garlic into a food processor along with any accumulated juices. Process until smooth.

Stored in a sealed glass jar in the refrigerator, Roasted Garlic Purée will keep for several weeks. That is, if you're slacking!

Tip: As a variation, add a few sprigs of fresh rosemary to the garlic before roasting.

Per tablespoon: calories: 34, protein: 1 g, fat: 1 g, carbohydrate: 6 g, fiber: 0 g, sodium: 36 mg, omega-3 fatty acids: 0 g

CHIPOTLE CHILE PURÉE

Makes about 1⅔ cups

A little dab of this fiery condiment will spice up any dish.

3 cans (7 ounces each) chipotles en adobo

Open the cans and dump the contents into a blender. Process on high to a smooth paste—depending on your blender, this could take 1 to 3 or maybe even 4 minutes. Press through a medium-mesh strainer to remove any un-blended seeds or skins. (Don't use a very fine mesh, as this will take forever and produce a virtually identical result.)

Stored in a glass jar in the refrigerator, Chipotle Chile Purée will keep for at least 3 weeks. (Actually, it will keep a lot longer. To tell the truth, I've never had any go bad on me, probably because nothing can live in it and only humans are interested in eating it. On the other hand, once you start using it and acquire a taste for it, this won't be an issue, believe me.)

Per tablespoon: calories: 6, protein: 0 g, fat: 0 g, carbohydrate: 1 g, fiber: 1 g, sodium: 150 mg, omega-3 fatty acids: 0 g

CHIPOTLE MAYONNAISE

Makes about 1⅓ cups

The chipotle chile stands out as a quintessential flavor, providing both heat and smoky depth to anything it touches. It's a staple in my kitchen, in dried and canned forms as well as in this mayonnaise. For those who are familiar with my first cookbook, *Omega-3 Cuisine*, it may seem like cheating to use an ingredient like prepared mayonnaise instead of making it from scratch. So what. The goal is speed, right?

> 1 cup vegan mayonnaise
> ⅓ cup Chipotle Chile Purée (page 40), or more, if you like the heat

Combine the mayonnaise and Chipotle Chile Purée in a small bowl. Whisk until well blended.

Stored in a sealed glass jar in the refrigerator, Chipotle Mayonnaise will keep for 2 weeks. (If it lasts longer than this, you're not using it often enough.)

Per serving: calories: 52, protein: 0 g, fat: 5 g, carbohydrate: 2 g, fiber: 0 g, sodium: 73 mg, omega-3 fatty acids: 0 g

HOT RED PEPPER SAUCE

Makes about 2 cups

This is a very useful sauce, and it keeps for well over a week in the refrigerator (not that it will last that long). You'll get totally respectable results with roasted peppers from a jar, so save yourself some time and trouble. If you prefer, vary the degree of heat by adjusting the amount of red chile powder, or omit it altogether for a mild red pepper sauce.

> 7 roasted red peppers
> 12 cloves peeled garlic
> 1 tablespoon hot red Indian chile powder or cayenne
> 1 teaspoon sea salt
> ¼ cup extra-virgin olive oil
> ¼ cup flax oil

Put the red peppers, garlic, chile powder, and salt in a blender. Process until smooth. With the motor running, slowly add the oils through the cap opening in the lid. Process until the mixture is an even light red color.

Stored in a sealed glass jar in the refrigerator, Hot Red Pepper Sauce will keep for 2 weeks.

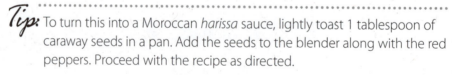

Tip: To turn this into a Moroccan *harissa* sauce, lightly toast 1 tablespoon of caraway seeds in a pan. Add the seeds to the blender along with the red peppers. Proceed with the recipe as directed.

Per tablespoon: calories: 37, protein: 0 g, fat: 3 g, carbohydrate: 1 g, fiber: 0 g, sodium: 68 mg, omega-3 fatty acids: 0 g

SUNDRIED TOMATO PASTE

Makes about 1¼ cups

This tomato paste is terrific for a number of uses. Add it to sauces, soups, and dips to pump up the flavor and complexity; use it as a sandwich spread; or add a little hot broth to it for a quick, light pasta sauce.

> 1 jar (8.5 ounces) marinated sundried tomatoes, thoroughly drained
> ½ to ¾ cup water, as needed
> 2 tablespoons extra-virgin olive oil
> 2 teaspoons minced or pressed garlic
> ½ teaspoon sea salt
> ¼ teaspoon freshly ground black pepper

Combine all the ingredients in a blender. Process until smooth.

Stored in a sealed glass jar in the refrigerator, Sundried Tomato Paste will keep for 1 month.

Per tablespoon: calories: 39, protein: 1 g, fat: 3 g, carbohydrate: 2 g, fiber: 1 g, sodium: 86 mg, omega-3 fatty acids: 0 g

BALSAMIC VINAIGRETTE

Makes about ¾ cup

If there is one salad dressing that merits being a standard pantry item, this is it. You can use it on a wide variety of salads, even coleslaw, with excellent results. If you have any garlic "issues," cut back on the quantity or omit it altogether; the vinaigrette will still be perfectly delicious. This recipe makes a small amount—enough to dress a salad for up to eight people. Once you've tried it, you might decide to double or even quadruple the recipe next time. For a creamier dressing, blast all the ingredients in a blender instead of merely whisking them.

    ¼ cup balsamic vinegar
    ¼ cup extra-virgin olive oil
    ¼ cup flax oil
    1 tablespoon Dijon mustard
    4 cloves peeled garlic, minced or pressed
    ½ teaspoon sea salt
    ¼ teaspoon freshly ground black pepper

Put all the ingredients in a small bowl. Whisk until emulsified.

    Stored in a sealed glass jar in the refrigerator, Balsamic Vinaigrette will keep for 1 month.

Per tablespoon: calories: 88, protein: 0 g, fat: 9 g, carbohydrate: 1 g, fiber: 0 g, sodium: 123 mg, omega-3 fatty acids: 2.4 g

ROSEMARY BALSAMIC DIPPING OIL

Makes about ¾ cup

This is a simple yet sophisticated condiment to have on the table for people to dip bread into. It is equally good as a splash on braised or steamed vegetables. You can even use it as a salad dressing.

4 cloves peeled garlic, lightly chopped
1 teaspoon sea salt
1 tablespoon coarsely chopped fresh rosemary leaves
½ cup extra-virgin olive oil
2 tablespoons balsamic vinegar
1 tablespoon finely chopped fresh parsley
½ teaspoon freshly ground black pepper

Pound the garlic in a mortar with the salt for about 1 minute, until a paste forms. Add the rosemary leaves and pound until they are fairly well pulverized and only small bits remain. Mash and stir in the oil with the pestle. Add the vinegar and continue mashing and stirring until the mixture has somewhat emulsified. Add the parsley and pepper and stir. Scrape into low, flat bowls and set out as a dip for crusty bread.

Stored in a sealed glass jar in the refrigerator, Rosemary Balsamic Dipping Oil will keep for 1 month.

Per tablespoon: calories: 84, protein: 0 g, fat: 9 g, carbohydrate: 1 g, fiber: 0 g, sodium: 179 mg, omega-3 fatty acids: 0 g

BROWN RICE CEREAL

Makes about 2 cups (about 6 servings)

In the early '70s, during my macrobiotic period, breakfast consisted of miso soup with seaweed, followed by a bowl of brown rice cereal with tahini and roasted sunflower seeds. Fond memories. Cooking this cereal represents an investment of time. First, the rice is toasted in a skillet, allowed to cool, and ground. Then it is added to boiling water and simmered for about 20 minutes. I recommend preparing a large batch of the toasted, ground rice at one time; then all you'll need to do in the morning is measure out a small portion and simmer it. So I've broken down the recipe into two separate parts: the pantry item and the breakfast item.

TOASTED AND GROUND BROWN RICE

2 cups short- or medium-grain brown rice

Pour the rice into a large, dry skillet over high heat. Stir and shake the pan to keep the rice moving so it will toast without burning. Toast the rice for about 10 minutes, or until it makes a few popping sounds and is aromatic. Immediately pour the rice onto a large tray or platter. Let it cool completely.

Working in small batches, pulse the rice in a blender, spice mill, or food processor until it turns into a grainy powder. Don't aim for a uniform, fine powder; about half of the mixture should still be in small pieces. (This will produce a much more interesting and pleasant-tasting cereal.)

Stored in an airtight container in the freezer, Toasted and Ground Brown Rice will keep indefinitely. Of course, if you use it often, this prognosis will never be tested. I always store rice in the freezer if I plan to keep it for any length of time to prevent its natural oils from turning rancid.

HOT BROWN RICE CEREAL

Makes 1 serving

2 cups water
⅓ cup Toasted and Ground Brown Rice
¼ teaspoon sea salt
1 to 3 tablespoons tahini
1 or 2 tablespoons toasted sunflower seeds
1 tablespoon natto miso (optional—but try it!)

Bring the water to a boil in a small pot. Whisk in the ground rice and salt. As soon as the mixture returns to a boil, turn the heat down to the lowest setting and cover the pot. Cook for about 20 minutes, checking often and stirring to keep the mixture from sticking. After 20 minutes, uncover, stir the mixture, and check the consistency. It should be just right, but if it's a little thin, increase the heat to medium-high and cook uncovered for a few minutes longer, stirring often. Taste to make sure it is cooked to your liking, and then remove it from the heat. Serve (or eat) right away, accompanied with the tahini, sunflower seeds, and natto miso.

Tip: If you like your cereal sweet, omit the natto miso and add 1 tablespoon of maple syrup.

Per serving: calories: 483, protein: 14 g, fat: 24 g, carbohydrate: 53 g, fiber: 7 g, sodium: 556 mg, omega-3 fatty acids: 0 g

SNACKS

HAZELNUT DIP

Makes about 4 servings

This is an ideal dip for pita bread, but it's even better served with raw vegetables, such as celery sticks (or fingers, if you're entertaining an informal crowd). Be sure to use a fresh, high-quality paprika.

1¼ cup hazelnuts
1 large tomato, coarsely chopped
¼ cup fresh parsley leaves
2 tablespoons sherry vinegar
2 tablespoons extra-virgin olive oil
2 tablespoons flax oil
4 cloves peeled garlic, minced or pressed
1 teaspoon Hungarian hot paprika
1 teaspoon sea salt
1 teaspoon agave nectar
½ teaspoon cayenne

Put the hazelnuts in a small bowl. Cover them with boiling water and let soak until cool. Drain, rinse under cold water, and drain again. This step will remove the bitterness from the skins and soften the nuts, without the need for overnight soaking. Spread the hazelnuts in a single layer on a towel to absorb the excess water.

Put the hazelnuts in a food processor and process until finely ground. Add the remaining ingredients and process until smooth. Transfer to a bowl or storage container and cover tightly. If time permits, refrigerate for at least 2 hours before serving to allow the flavors to develop.

Stored in a covered container in the refrigerator, Hazelnut Dip will keep for 2 to 3 days.

Per serving: calories: 437, protein: 8 g, fat: 42 g, carbohydrate: 7 g, fiber: 5 g, sodium: 38 mg, omega-3 fatty acids: 3.6 g

EGYPTIAN EGGPLANT

Makes 4 servings

I once worked for an Egyptian gentleman who professed a passionate hatred of garlic, but he adored this dish. I learned a number of Egyptian dishes to please his palate, and although most of them were loaded with garlic, he loved them all. Such is the power of delicious food—like love, it can overcome prejudice and hatred.

- 2 eggplants
- 4 cloves peeled garlic
- ½ teaspoon sea salt
- 1 tablespoon sesame seeds
- ¼ cup extra-virgin olive oil
- 2 tablespoons chopped fresh parsley
- 1 tablespoon freshly squeezed lemon juice
- ¼ teaspoon freshly ground black pepper
- Toast points or flatbread

Preheat a grill (preferably an outdoor charcoal grill). Put the whole eggplants on the hot grill and cook, turning often, for 15 to 20 minutes, or until they are soft and charred all over.

While the eggplants are cooking, mash the garlic with the salt in a mortar to form a mushy paste. Add the sesame seeds and mash lightly. Add the olive oil and mash everything together. Stir in the parsley, lemon juice, and pepper. Set aside until the eggplants are done.

Transfer the eggplants to a large plate or cutting board and cut them in half lengthwise. Scoop out the flesh, avoiding as much of the charred skin as possible (some will get into the mix, but that's okay—it will add a nice flavor), and put it in a bowl. Add the reserved garlic mixture. Stir well, mashing any large pieces of eggplant. Serve with toast points or flatbread.

Per serving: calories: 153, protein: 1 g, fat: 15 g, carbohydrate: 3 g, fiber: 3 g, sodium: 270 mg, omega-3 fatty acids: 0.1 g

PAPADUMS WITH FRESH GREEN CHUTNEY

Makes 4 to 6 servings (See photo between pages 86 and 87.)

Papadums, made from lentils, are like Indian tapas, and they are one of the absolute best bar snacks in the world. Their usual accompaniment is a pair of chutneys—a spicy green one and a sweet tamarind one. The green chutney is made with fresh coriander, green chiles, and sometimes mint. It's a brilliant condiment for perking up virtually any meal, especially one with an Asian flavor.

> 1 package papadums (about 12)
> 2 cups packed fresh cilantro leaves, coarsely chopped
> 1 red onion, coarsely chopped
> 1 cup packed mint leaves, coarsely chopped
> ¼ cup freshly squeezed lemon juice
> 7 cloves peeled garlic, coarsely chopped
> 1 (2-inch) piece fresh ginger, peeled and thinly sliced across the grain
> 4 hot green chiles, or more for increased heat
> 1 teaspoon sea salt

Remove the papadums from the package and carefully separate them. Turn a gas stove burner on and, using tongs, pass each papadum back and forth over the open flame, alternating front and back. This should be done in a slow, even motion, so that the heat is intense enough to make the papadum puff slightly and create a lightly toasted, rumpled surface, without burning. As one side is done, switch to holding the other end and continue until the entire papadum is uniformly puffed and toasted. Proceed with the remaining papadums in the same way, stacking them on a plate or in a napkin-lined basket. If you do not have a gas stove, papadums can also be puffed by slipping them into a small pan of hot oil, one at a time. They will puff all at once. Remove them quickly to prevent burning and drain them on a towel.

To make the chutney, put the cilantro, onion, mint, lemon juice, garlic, ginger, chilies, and salt in a blender. Process until smooth, stopping to scrape down the sides of the blender jar as needed. Pour into a small bowl. Serve the chutney as a dip with the toasted papadums.

Tip: If mint proves hard to find, use all cilantro. Fresh chutney is best used right away. However, although you definitely will notice a difference in the chutney's taste and color when it has been stored for a day, it will still be enjoyable. Keep refrigerated.

Per serving: calories: 212, protein: 9 g, fat: 1 g, carbohydrate: 41 g, fiber: 10 g, sodium: 1,139 mg, omega-3 fatty acids: 0.36 g

ARTICHOKE SANDWICH SPREAD

Makes about 1 cup

For something so fast and so simple, this spread has a pretty sophisticated flavor and texture. It goes very well with multigrain bread, sundried tomatoes, and Sicilian olives. To use it as a dip, just double the mayonnaise and process it a little longer.

¾ cup artichoke hearts (packed in water), pressed to thoroughly drain
¼ cup vegan mayonnaise
1 small shallot, lightly chopped
1 teaspoon freshly squeezed lemon juice
1 teaspoon truffle-infused virgin olive oil (optional)
¼ teaspoon sea salt
¼ teaspoon freshly ground black pepper

Put all the ingredients in a food processor. Pulse just until the vegetables are finely chopped. Some texture is desirable, so stop and check frequently to avoid overprocessing.

Stored in a sealed glass container in the refrigerator, Artichoke Sandwich Spread will keep for 3 to 4 days.

Per 3 tablespoons: calories: 78, protein: 1 g, fat: 5 g, carbohydrate: 6 g, fiber: 1 g, sodium: 291 mg, omega-3 fatty acids: 0 g

HOT EGGPLANT AND SEITAN OPEN-FACE SANDWICHES

Makes 4 servings   (See photo facing page 86.)

I was imagining possible ways to use seitan when this combination came to me. Even my eighty-four-year-old mother enjoyed it. If you have any fresh shiitake mushrooms, they would go well too; slice them and add them to the sauce.

    1 medium-size eggplant
    3 tablespoons almond or extra-virgin olive oil
    2 teaspoons toasted sesame oil
    ¼ teaspoon sea salt
    1 cup tomato purée
    ¼ cup hoisin sauce
    1 tablespoon dark agave nectar
    8 ounces seitan, cut into ½-inch-thick slices
    4 large slices sourdough bread or your favorite French bread
    8 scallions, thinly sliced
    1 tablespoon sesame seeds

Preheat the oven to 450 degrees F. Put a baking pan on the middle rack.

Heat a stovetop grill over high heat.

Prepare the eggplant while the oven and grill are heating. Cut a lengthwise strip off both sides of the eggplant to expose the flesh. Cut the eggplant into 4 thick slices parallel to the cut sides. Combine the almond oil with 1 teaspoon of the sesame oil in a small bowl. Brush the eggplant slices very lightly on both sides with about half of the oil mixture. Arrange them in a single layer on a plate or tray. Sprinkle both sides of the eggplant slices with the salt.

Put the eggplant on the hot grill and cook for about 5 minutes on each side. Transfer the eggplant to the baking pan in the oven. Keep the grill hot.

To make the sauce, combine the tomato purée, hoisin sauce, agave nectar, and remaining teaspoon of sesame oil in a small saucepan over medium heat.

Toss the seitan slices with the remaining oil mixture. Put them on the grill and cook for about 3 minutes on each side.

Add the seitan to the sauce and stir well. Decrease the heat to keep the sauce and seitan hot but not bubbling.

Toast the bread slices and put one slice on each plate. Put an eggplant slice on each piece of toast. Divide the hot seitan and sauce among the 4 slices, covering the eggplant. Sprinkle with the scallions and sesame seeds. Serve at once.

Per serving: calories: 485, protein: 49 g, fat: 15 g, carbohydrate: 37 g, fiber: 5 g, sodium: 646 mg, omega-3 fatty acids: 0.08 g

TEMPEH STICKS WITH PEANUT SAUCE

Makes about 4 servings   (See photo between pages 86 and 87.)

Tempeh was a hard sell for me. A good friend who has been part of the grand vegan experiment since the sixties and who is also an expert in tempeh culture put me up to trying it. I had a few dismal failures before coming up with this recipe. Even my sixteen-year-old son liked it (and even after I told him what it was, he *still* liked it).

½ cup coconut milk
¼ cup chopped fresh cilantro
2 tablespoons Sriracha sauce
1 tablespoon peeled and chopped fresh ginger
1 tablespoon agave nectar
1 stalk lemongrass (outer leaf removed), finely chopped
¼ teaspoon sea salt
½ cup dry-roasted unsalted peanuts
8 ounces tempeh
¼ cup coconut oil

To make the sauce, combine the coconut milk, cilantro, Sriracha sauce, ginger, agave nectar, lemongrass, and salt in a blender. Process until smooth. Add the peanuts. Pulse until thick, with a few small peanut pieces remaining. Pour into a small bowl.

To make the tempeh sticks, cut the tempeh into ¼-inch-thick slices. Heat the coconut oil in a sauté pan and add a layer of the tempeh slices. Cook until lightly browned on one side. Turn the tempeh slices over and lightly brown the other side. Transfer to a paper towel and blot the excess oil. Repeat with the remaining tempeh slices.

Place the bowl of sauce on the side of a plate and arrange the tempeh sticks in front of it. Serve at once. Mmmm.

Per serving: calories: 413, protein: 16 g, fat: 35 g, carbohydrate: 10 g, fiber: 5 g, sodium: 199 g, omega-3 fatty acids: 0 g

SOUPS

PIMIENTO SOUP WITH VERMOUTH

Makes about 4 servings   (See photo between pages 86 and 87.)

The slightly bitter character of vermouth adds a layer of flavor complexity that enhances the pimientos dramatically. With a mere tablespoon of olive oil, this is an amazingly rich soup, reminiscent of classic tomato bisque but without the hassle. Very sexy. I recommend serving it in small teacups as a starter for an elegant dinner. If you don't like to use alcohol in your food, simply omit this ingredient and call it "Pimiento Soup," which will be an unusual, very tasty dish all the same.

> 1 tablespoon extra-virgin olive oil
> 1 yellow or white onion, finely diced
> 9 cloves peeled garlic, finely chopped
> 1½ cups (three 4-ounce jars) pimientos, rinsed, drained, and
>   coarsely chopped
> 2 vegetable bouillon cubes
> 1 teaspoon smoked paprika
> 4 cups water
> ½ teaspoon sea salt
> 1 small russet potato
> ¼ cup dry vermouth, preferably Noilly Prat (optional)
> ¼ teaspoon freshly ground black pepper
> 1 teaspoon snipped fresh chives

Put the oil in a large soup pot over high heat. Add the onion and cook and stir for 1 minute. Add the garlic and cook and stir for about 1 minute. Add the pimientos, bouillon cubes, and paprika and cook and stir for 1 minute. Add the water and salt and bring to a boil.

Peel the potato, and then grate it directly into the pot. Stir well. Decrease the heat to medium-high and simmer for 10 to 15 minutes, or until the vegetables are very tender. The liquid should be reduced to about 1½ cups.

Transfer the mixture to a blender and process until very smooth. (Be careful, as the hot mixture may want to blast out of the blender. Pulse a few times before turning the blender on fully.)

Return to the pot and reheat. When the soup is hot, add the vermouth, if using, and pepper and stir well. The consistency should be very creamy, but if the soup is too thick, add just a little water. Serve in small cups, with a sprinkling of the chives on top.

Per serving: calories: 120, protein: 2 g, fat: 3 g, carbohydrate: 19 g, fiber: 3 g, sodium: 310 mg, omega-3 fatty acids: 0.03 g

LEEK AND PARSNIP SOUP

Makes about 6 servings

While many people have ignored parsnips, perhaps because of their appearance (they look a bit like misshapen, anemic carrots), I would encourage the wary to try them at least once. Their flavor is very special, much more interesting than a carrot's.

Leeks, as you may know, are a member of the *Allium* family, which includes garlic, onions, shallots, and scallions (in decreasing order of intensity). I mention this because it's a fabulously pungent family, well suited to sautéing and braising, both of which concentrate and mellow the character of these vegetables, providing a rich flavor base for many sauces, soups, and other dishes. In combination with sweet root vegetables such as carrots, or in this case, parsnips, the result is rather mild and delectable. Chives are also in the *Allium* family, but because their flavor is so subtle, they are always served raw and freshly cut, as a mild flavor and visual enhancer, and added at the last possible moment.

> 2 tablespoons extra-virgin olive oil
> ½ cup finely diced shallots
> 2 leeks (white and green parts), finely diced (see tip)
> 2 cloves peeled garlic, crushed
> 1½ pounds parsnips, peeled and grated
> 8 cups water
> 1½ teaspoons sea salt
> 2 vegetable bouillon cubes
> ¼ teaspoon freshly ground black pepper
> ¼ teaspoon mace
> 1 tablespoon snipped fresh chives

Heat the oil in a large soup pot. Add the shallots and cook, stirring constantly to prevent them from browning, for 1 to 2 minutes, until they release their fragrant aroma. Add the leeks and garlic, stirring until they are limp and fragrant, about 1 to 2 minutes. Add the parsnips and cook and stir until the mixture is almost dry, about 4 minutes longer. Add the water, salt, and bouillon cubes and bring to a boil. Decrease the heat and simmer for about 15 minutes, or until the vegetables are tender. Remove from the heat.

Working in small batches, transfer the soup to a blender and process until completely smooth. Return the soup to the pot. Season with the pepper and mace. Taste and add more salt, if needed. Warm over medium-low heat. Serve at once, garnished with the chives.

Tip: Leeks typically contain a lot of grit and sand. To clean them, slice each leek lengthwise, leaving the root end intact to hold the leaves in place. Rinse well under running water, gently spreading the leaves apart and rubbing to loosen any stubborn dirt. Drain well, cut off the root end, and proceed with the recipe.

Per serving: calories: 162, protein: 3 g, fat: 5 g, carbohydrate: 24 g, fiber: 6 g, sodium: 572 mg, omega-3 fatty acids: 0.03 g

LEEK AND CAULIFLOWER SOUP

Makes about 6 servings   (See photo between pages 86 and 87.)

Cauliflower and curry flavors go well together, which in this case is hinted at by the addition of ras el hanout, a Moroccan spice mixture slightly reminiscent of Indian curry but uniquely North African in character. Feel free to substitute an Indian curry powder for the ras el hanout in this recipe—it will be delicious either way.

> 1 head cauliflower
> 3 tablespoons extra-virgin olive oil
> 4 leeks (white and green parts), finely diced (see tip, page 61)
> 1 potato, peeled and finely diced
> 7 cloves peeled garlic, chopped
> 1 tablespoon ras el hanout or Indian curry powder
> 1 teaspoon sea salt
> 1 quart water
> 3 vegetables bouillon cubes
> 1 cup fresh or frozen peas
> ¼ cup chopped fresh cilantro

Break the cauliflower into small florets, reserving the very smallest ones separately from the rest (about 1 cup).

Heat the oil in a large soup pot. Add the leeks, potato, and cauliflower (except for the reserved cup of very small florets). Cook and stir for 1 to 2 minutes, until the vegetables begin to release their juices. Add the garlic, ras el hanout, and salt. Decrease the heat and cook and stir until the mixture is almost dry, about 3 minutes. Add the water and bouillon cubes. Increase the heat to high and bring to a boil. Decrease the heat and simmer for about 15 minutes, or until the vegetables are tender.

While the soup is cooking, bring a small pot of water to a boil over high heat. Add the peas and the reserved cup of cauliflower florets. Decrease the heat slightly and cook until just tender, about 5 minutes. Drain and reserve.

When the leeks, potato, and cauliflower are tender, remove from the heat. Working in small batches, process the vegetables and their cooking liquid in a blender. Return the blended mixture to the pot. Stir in the reserved cauliflower and peas.

Warm the soup over medium-low heat. Taste and add more salt, if needed. Stir in the cilantro. Serve at once.

Per serving: calories: 164, protein: 5 g, fat: 5 g, carbohydrate: 22 g, fiber: 6 g, sodium: 444 mg, omega-3 fatty acids: 0.03 g

NAVY BEAN AND SWISS CHARD SOUP

Makes about 4 servings

The canned beans in this recipe are already cooked, which allows you to make an unusual bean soup with barely cooked vegetables (which I like) in about thirty minutes. If (like my wife) you prefer more tender vegetables, all you'll need to do is cover the soup and leave it over medium-low heat for an additional fifteen to twenty minutes. Either way, it's a very satisfying dish.

        1 bunch Swiss chard
        2 tablespoons extra-virgin olive oil
        1 large onion, diced
        7 cloves peeled garlic, finely chopped
        2 vegetable bouillon cubes
        1 teaspoon smoked paprika or Hungarian hot paprika
        ½ teaspoon sea salt
        4 cups water
        2 cans (15 ounces each) white navy beans, rinsed and drained

Separate the Swiss chard leaves from the stems and wash well. Chop the leaves coarsely and set them aside. Cut the stems into strips lengthwise, and then slice them crosswise into small dice.

Put the oil in a large soup pot over high heat. Add the onion and cook and stir for 1 minute. Add the garlic and chard stems and cook and stir for about 1 minute. Stir in the chard leaves. As they begin to wilt, add the bouillon cubes, paprika, and salt. Cook and stir for 1 minute. Add the water and bring to a boil. Decrease the heat, cover, and simmer for about 10 minutes, or until the vegetables are just barely tender. Add the beans and warm through. Remove from the heat and serve at once.

Per serving: calories: 353, protein: 16 g, fat: 8 g, carbohydrate: 35 g, fiber: 21 g, sodium: 372 mg, omega-3 fatty acids: 0.05 g

TUSCAN KALE AND COCONUT SOUP WITH TOFU

Makes about 4 servings

This was inspired by the wonderful Thai coconut soup *Tom Kha Kai*, which I've left behind because it features both chicken and fish sauce. No problem—I'll make my own coconut soups! Tuscan kale, also called lacinato kale, looks more like a small, dark green variety of Swiss chard than kale, but it takes longer to cook than chard, which actually makes it ideal for this soup. If you keep broccoli stalks instead of throwing them out (or composting them), this is one good use for them.

> 1 tablespoon almond or sesame oil
> 1 medium-size red onion, diced
> 1 bunch Tuscan kale (stems removed), coarsely chopped
> 3 broccoli stalks, peeled and thinly sliced
> 1/4 cup Thai green curry paste
> 3 cups water
> 2 cans (13.5 ounces each) Thai coconut milk
> 2 vegetable bouillon cubes
> 8 ounces firm silken tofu, cut into small cubes
> 1 bunch fresh cilantro, coarsely chopped
> 1 tablespoon freshly squeezed lime juice

Put the oil in a large soup pot over medium-high heat. Add the onion and cook and stir for 1 minute. Add the kale, broccoli stalks, and curry paste and cook and stir for about 1 minute. Add the water, coconut milk, and bouillon cubes and bring to a boil. Immediately decrease the heat and simmer for about 10 minutes, or until the vegetables are tender.

Add the tofu and warm through. Add the cilantro and lime juice and stir well. Remove from the heat and serve at once.

Per serving: calories: 525, protein: 12 g, fat: 46 g, carbohydrate: 18 g, fiber: 3 g, sodium: 355 mg, omega-3 fatty acids: 0 g

WHITE BEAN SOUP WITH TUSCAN KALE

Makes about 4 to 6 servings

The smell of beans cooking is intoxicating for me, but we'll have to forgo that in favor of speed (great-a granda-mamma forgive-a me). Tuscan kale is more delicate than regular kale, but if you can't find any, go ahead and substitute the regular kind, no worries. Just to make sure we keep this under thirty minutes, start boiling the water before you do your prep; that way, you'll be ahead of the game when it comes time to add it. This soup is best served with a crusty Italian—bread, that is.

6 cups water
2 stalks celery, coarsely chopped
1 medium-size red onion, coarsely chopped
1 carrot, coarsely chopped
7 cloves peeled garlic
3 tablespoons extra-virgin olive oil
1 bunch Tuscan kale (stems removed), coarsely chopped
3 vegetable bouillon cubes
1 teaspoon sea salt
2 cans (15 ounces each) cannellini beans, rinsed and drained
1 tablespoon agave nectar, if needed
1 tablespoon chopped fresh parsley

Pour the water into a medium pot and bring to a boil over medium-high heat.

Put the celery, onion, carrot, and garlic in a food processor. Pulse until very finely chopped.

Put the oil in a large soup pot over medium-high heat. Add the onion mixture from the food processor, stirring well. Cook, stirring often to prevent sticking (followed by burning), for about 3 minutes. Add the kale and stir until wilted. Add the boiling water, bouillon cubes, and salt. Bring to a boil, decrease the heat, and simmer for about 15 minutes, or until the kale is tender. Add the beans and simmer until heated through.

Taste and adjust the seasonings, if needed. If you detect an unwelcome bitter edge, add the agave nectar. Remove from the heat and stir in the parsley. Serve at once.

Per serving: calories: 326, protein: 14g, fat: 9 g, carbohydrate: 34 g, fiber: 16 g, sodium: 510 mg, omega-3 fatty acids: 0.06 g

SALADS

BEET AND CELERY ROOT SALAD

Makes 4 to 6 servings

This visually stunning salad is a meal that will fill you up but won't weigh you down. If you have trouble locating both arugula and watercress, simply use a double quantity of whichever one you find. I like to cut the vegetables into very fine julienne (thin as matchsticks), but if this seems too taxing, just grate them. If you can't find celery root, substitute with celery stalks, peeled and cut the same way.

 1 bunch arugula
 1 bunch watercress
 1 large beet
 1 small celery root
 1 tart apple
 1 small red onion
 $\frac{1}{3}$ cup freshly squeezed lemon juice
 2 tablespoons Roasted Garlic Purée (page 39)
 1 tablespoon Dijon mustard
 1 tablespoon agave nectar
 $\frac{1}{2}$ teaspoon sea salt
 $\frac{1}{4}$ teaspoon freshly ground black pepper
 $\frac{1}{4}$ cup extra-virgin olive oil
 $\frac{1}{4}$ cup flax oil
 $\frac{1}{2}$ cup broken walnuts

Remove any coarse stems from the arugula and wash in plenty of water along with the watercress leaves. Allow the greens to soak and crisp while you prepare the rest of the salad.

Peel the beet, celery root, and apple. Cut them into fine julienne or coarsely grate them. Cut the onion in half lengthwise, and then thinly slice it crosswise.

Combine the lemon juice, Roasted Garlic Purée, mustard, agave nectar, salt, and pepper in a large bowl. Whisk until well blended. Whisk in the olive and flax oils and continue whisking until emulsified. Add the julienned vegetables and toss until well coated. Let sit for about 5 minutes.

Drain the arugula and watercress. Dry it in a salad spinner or roll it gently in a towel to absorb the excess water. Add to the vegetables and toss well. Divide among 4 to 6 plates. Sprinkle the walnuts on top. Serve at once.

Per serving: calories: 339, protein: 4 g, fat: 29 g, carbohydrate: 15 g, fiber: 3 g, sodium: 336 mg, omega-3 fatty acids: 5.76 g

FENNEL VINAIGRETTE

Makes about 1 cup

I love bright green dressings. This one came about when I was preparing some fennel for Salad of Fennel, Roasted Peppers, and Romaine Hearts (page 102) and had no immediate use for the fronds, which were very fresh and attractive. Suddenly it came to me that this would be the ideal dressing for a salad featuring fennel. That may sound like a no-brainer, but I usually try to create a flavor counterpoint in salads, so the idea was somewhat unorthodox for me. On the other hand, I am somewhat unorthodox myself, so maybe this was, well, oddly orthodox. Whatever.

½ cup chopped and packed fennel fronds
¼ cup white balsamic vinegar
4 cloves peeled garlic
2 teaspoons Dijon mustard
½ teaspoon sea salt
¼ teaspoon freshly ground black pepper
½ cup extra-virgin olive oil

Put the fennel fronds, vinegar, garlic, mustard, salt, and pepper in a blender. Process on high speed until smooth, stopping once or twice to scrape down the sides of the blender jar with a spatula. With the motor running, slowly add the oil in a thin stream through the cap opening in the lid. Use at once.

Per tablespoon: calories: 66, protein: 0 g, fat: 7 g, carbohydrate: 1 g, fiber: 0 g, sodium: 85 mg, omega-3 fatty acids: 0.05 g

CANNELLINI SALAD WITH LEMON VINAIGRETTE

Makes 4 to 6 servings

This is an ideal one-dish dinner for a warm summer evening. Despite the long list of ingredients, it's surprisingly quick to make.

- 1 can (15 ounces) cannellini beans, rinsed and drained
- 3 small zucchini, grated
- 3 stalks celery, thinly sliced
- 1 red onion, thinly sliced
- 1 beet, scrubbed or peeled and grated
- 2 roasted red peppers, quartered and sliced
- 4 radishes, quartered and sliced
- 1 bunch watercress
- ½ head iceberg lettuce, cut into 1-inch cubes
- ¼ cup freshly squeezed lemon juice
- ¼ cup extra-virgin olive oil
- ¼ cup flax oil
- 4 cloves peeled garlic, pressed
- ½ teaspoon sea salt
- ½ teaspoon freshly ground black pepper

Combine the beans, zucchini, celery, onion, beet, red peppers, and radishes in a large bowl. Toss well. Place the watercress and lettuce on top.

Combine the lemon juice, olive oil, flax oil, garlic, salt, and pepper in a small bowl and whisk until emulsified. Pour over the vegetables. Toss gently but thoroughly. Serve at once.

Per serving: calories: 293, protein: 6 g, fat: 22 g, carbohydrate: 15 g, fiber: 5 g, sodium: 263 mg, omega-3 fatty acids: 5.76 g

GRETA'S CANNELLINI SALAD WITH MINT

Makes about 4 servings

A dear friend of mine, knowing that I was writing this book, told me about this quick and easy salad. It didn't sound too spectacular, but I trust her impeccable taste, so I tried it. It turned out to be a brilliant salad, with a sophisticated combination of flavors and textures. The buttery, subtle character of cannellini beans cannot be duplicated, but in a pinch, you can substitute with regular white navy beans with tolerable results. Just don't skimp on the mint! This salad is best served immediately, at room temperature, but it can also be refrigerated and served the following day.

1 can (15 ounces) cannellini beans, rinsed and drained
¾ cup finely diced red onion
¾ cup coarsely chopped fresh mint
3 tablespoons extra-virgin olive oil
2 tablespoons freshly squeezed lemon juice
¼ teaspoon sea salt
¼ teaspoon freshly ground black pepper

Combine all the ingredients in a large bowl. Serve at once, in small bowls.

Per serving: calories: 169, protein: 5 g, fat: 10 g, carbohydrate: 12 g, fiber: 4 g, sodium: 139 mg, omega-3 fatty acids: 0.08 g

CUCUMBERS WITH POMEGRANATE VINAIGRETTE

Makes 4 to 8 servings

Although the quantity of this salad is enough for eight moderate servings, the taste is so intriguing that when I put out a platter of it for the first time, four people quickly polished it off. So if you want to control the portions, you'll have to serve it in small bowls.

> 4 cucumbers
> ¼ cup coarsely chopped fresh cilantro
> ¼ cup flax oil or extra-virgin olive oil
> 3 tablespoons pomegranate molasses
> 2 tablespoons freshly squeezed lemon juice
> 1 tablespoon Dijon mustard
> 7 cloves peeled garlic, pressed or pounded to a paste in a mortar with the salt
> ½ teaspoon sea salt
> ½ teaspoon toasted cumin seeds, ground (see tip)
> ¼ teaspoon Indian hot red chile powder or cayenne

Peel the cucumbers and cut them in half lengthwise. If the seeds are coarse, shove them out with your thumbnail or with a spoon. Cut the cucumbers into ⅜-inch-thick slices. Transfer them to a large bowl and add the cilantro.

If you are going to pound the garlic to a paste with the salt, do this first. Otherwise, combine the oil, pomegranate molasses, lemon juice, mustard, pressed garlic, salt, cumin, and chile powder in a small bowl and whisk until emulsified. Pour over the cucumbers and cilantro and toss well. Serve at once.

 Tip: There are two ways to prepare the toasted cumin seeds. The best way is to toast the whole seeds in a dry pan, shaking the pan constantly, until they turn slightly brown and release their fragrant aroma. Then pound them in a mortar. The other way is to toast ½ teaspoon of ground cumin the same way (no pounding required). The first way is much better for two reasons: one, whole spices always have a better flavor than preground spices; and two, when you pound the seeds by hand, you can control how finely they are ground. For this recipe, it is preferable to leave a few coarse pieces so they can release their flavor as you bite into them.

Per serving: calories: 133, protein: 1 g, fat: 9 g, carbohydrate: 13 g, fiber: 1 g, sodium: 234 mg, omega-3 fatty acids: 4.37 g

BLANCHED BEAN SPROUT SALAD

Makes 4 servings

This variation of a Korean dish is almost lightning quick. A brief blanching of the bean sprouts renders them tender-crisp, and at the same time allows them to combine with the dressing better than they would raw, as you'll see. This salad is best served warm.

- 1 pound mung bean sprouts
- 4 scallions, very thinly sliced
- 3 tablespoons tamari
- 1 teaspoon toasted sesame oil

Fill a large pot with water and bring to a boil over high heat. Remove from the heat and drop the sprouts into the water. Stir once, and then immediately drain well in a colander, shaking firmly. Transfer the sprouts to a large platter. Add most of the scallions, reserving some of the green portion for a garnish, and toss. Spread out in a fairly even layer on the platter.

Combine the tamari and sesame oil in a small bowl and stir well. Drizzle over the sprouts. Sprinkle the reserved scallions on top. Serve at once or at room temperature.

Per serving: calories: 59, protein: 5 g, fat: 1 g, carbohydrate: 6 g, fiber: 2 g, sodium: 710 mg, omega-3 fatty acids: 0 g

CELERIAC RÉMOULADE

Makes 4 servings

Celeriac is also known as celery root. Often you will find that they are some-what porous inside, so always pick one that feels heavy, which indicates that it's fairly solid. This is especially important for any dish for which the celeriac is grated and served raw, as it is in this one. Also bear in mind that all of the outer skin must be pared away, leaving only the white inner flesh. Therefore, it's bet-ter to pick two smaller, less gnarly roots than one large one. Cornichons (very small, savory-sweet, French pickled cucumbers) are the traditional pickles used for rémoulade, but in a pinch you can substitute with regular supermarket-variety sweet pickles. Serve the rémoulade on its own, in small bowls, or on a bed of mixed greens.

   1½ pounds celeriac
   1 lemon, cut in half crosswise
   ½ cup vegan mayonnaise
   2 tablespoons finely chopped cornichons
   2 tablespoons capers, well rinsed and finely chopped
   2 tablespoons snipped fresh chives
   2 tablespoons chopped fresh parsley
   2 tablespoons finely chopped fresh chervil (optional)
   1 tablespoon finely chopped fresh tarragon
   1 tablespoon Dijon mustard

Peel the celeriac down to the white flesh. Rub it all over with the cut lemon, squeezing just a bit of juice as you go. This will prevent discoloration. Cut the celeriac into quarters and again, rub each piece all over with the lemon. Coarsely grate the celeriac and put it in a bowl. Immediately add the remaining ingredients and toss until evenly distributed. It's important to work quickly to prevent the grated celeriac from oxidizing and turning brown. Cover the bowl with plastic wrap and refrigerate until thoroughly chilled.

Per serving: calories: 228, protein: 3 g, fat: 15 g, carbohydrate: 21 g, fiber: 4 g, sodium: 549 mg, omega-3 fatty acids: 0 g

COOL-AND-SPICY SALAD

Makes 4 servings

Cucumber is a cooling vegetable (well, technically it's a fruit), and when combined with iceberg lettuce, it makes a perfect match for the spicy shallot vinaigrette in this speedy summer salad.

5 tablespoons flax oil
¼ to ⅓ cup finely diced shallots
3 tablespoons brown rice vinegar
1 to 2 tablespoons Sriracha sauce
1 tablespoon agave nectar
2 teaspoons minced garlic
½ teaspoon sea salt
¼ teaspoon freshly ground black pepper
1 English cucumber
½ head iceberg lettuce, cut into 1-inch chunks
2 tablespoons coarsely chopped fresh cilantro

To make the vinaigrette, combine the oil, shallots, vinegar, Sriracha sauce, agave nectar, garlic, salt, and pepper in a bowl. Whisk until emulsified. Set aside to allow the flavors to blend and develop while you prepare the vegetables.

To make the salad, peel the cucumber and score the entire surface lengthwise with a fork. Cut it in half lengthwise, and then cut each half diagonally into long slices about ¼ inch thick. Transfer to a large bowl. Add the lettuce, cilantro, and reserved vinaigrette. Toss until thoroughly distributed. Serve at once.

Per serving: calories: 211, protein: 2 g, fat: 17 g, carbohydrate: 12 g, fiber: 1 g, sodium: 571 mg, omega-3 fatty acids: 9 g

CRUNCHY VEGAN GODDESS

Makes 4 servings

The vegetables are crunchy (not the goddess), and the dressing is a veganized version of the classic American favorite, green goddess. I like the title, but of course when you make it, you can call it anything you want. I used a vegan yogurt made from coconut milk for this that produced a light, creamy dressing. You may wish to use another vegan yogurt for this, such as soy. It's best to make the dressing ahead of time and let it rest in the refrigerator for at least an hour for the flavors to fully develop, so I recommend preparing the salad veggies at the same time. That way, all you'll need to do is toss the dressing into the salad and you'll be ready to eat.

½ cup vegan mayonnaise
¼ cup vegan plain yogurt
3 tablespoons minced scallion greens or fresh chives
2 tablespoons minced fresh parsley
2 teaspoons minced fresh tarragon
2 teaspoons cider vinegar
2 teaspoons freshly squeezed lemon juice
⅛ teaspoon sea salt
⅛ teaspoon freshly ground black pepper
1 small head iceberg lettuce, cut into 1-inch chunks
3 stalks celery, thinly sliced on a diagonal
2 carrots, finely julienned or grated
½ red onion, thinly sliced
5 radishes, halved and thinly sliced

To make the dressing, put the mayonnaise, yogurt, scallion greens, parsley, tarragon, vinegar, lemon juice, salt, and pepper in a bowl. Whisk until thoroughly combined. Let rest in the refrigerator while you prepare the salad vegetables, or, time permitting, for at least an hour.

Put the lettuce, celery, carrots, onion, and radishes in a large bowl. If you are preparing the vegetables in advance, cover the bowl and refrigerate until serving time. When you are ready to serve the salad, add the dressing and toss well. Serve at once.

Per serving: calories: 182, protein: 2 g, fat: 14 g, carbohydrate: 11 g, fiber: 3 g, sodium: 231 mg, omega-3 fatty acids: 0 g

CURLY ENDIVE SALAD WITH PAPAYA

Makes 4 to 6 servings

Endive has a bitter edge, but it is instantly tamed by just a few bites here and there of red papaya and a sharp, citrusy vinaigrette. The salted black beans are optional, but they do add a layer of action and saltiness that rounds out the flavors nicely. For the best result, use mainly the tender inner greens of the endive for this salad. I know the list of ingredients looks scary, but don't be intimidated! This is one dish that takes well under thirty minutes.

6 cups curly endive greens (2 to 3 heads)
2 roasted red peppers, cut into strips
1 bunch scallions, thinly sliced on a diagonal
1 small red papaya, cut into ½-inch dice
2 tablespoons chopped fresh cilantro (optional)
2 tablespoons white balsamic or unseasoned rice vinegar
2 tablespoons freshly squeezed lime juice
1 tablespoon orange juice
1 tablespoon agave nectar
2 teaspoons Dijon mustard
2 teaspoons Chinese salted black beans, rinsed (optional)
1 teaspoon finely grated lime or lemon zest
1 teaspoon Sriracha sauce
½ teaspoon sea salt
¼ teaspoon freshly ground black pepper
½ cup extra-virgin olive oil
4 fresh basil leaves, shredded (optional)
1 tablespoon sesame seeds

To make the salad, combine the endive, red peppers, scallions, papaya, and cilantro, if using, in a large bowl.

To make the dressing, combine the vinegar, lime juice, orange juice, agave nectar, mustard, salted black beans, if using, lime zest, Sriracha sauce, salt, and pepper in a small bowl. Whisk until well blended. Add the oil, whisking constantly to form a light emulsion. Taste and adjust the seasonings, if needed. Stir in the basil leaves, if using.

Pour the dressing over the salad and toss gently but thoroughly. Sprinkle with the sesame seeds. Serve at once.

Per serving: calories: 272, protein: 2 g, fat: 23 g, carbohydrate: 12 g, fiber: 4 g, sodium: 338 mg, omega-3 fatty acids: 0.16 g

DANDELION AND RED ONION SALAD WITH BASIL VINAIGRETTE

Makes 4 servings

Dandelion greens are jam-packed with nutrients. When I lived in Switzerland, I would always see elders out in the fields during springtime picking wild dandelion greens before they passed the flowering stage. Smart people, the Swiss. Fortunately, dandelion greens are now widely available in many natural food stores and even some supermarkets. The sweet-sharp taste of red onion offsets the slightly bitter edge of the greens just enough to bring out the subtle aromatics in this salad, and it's all punctuated by little explosions of juicy grape tomatoes. If you want to make the preparation even speedier, substitute splashes of balsamic vinegar and olive oil for the dressing, with just a dash of sea salt and a few twists of the pepper mill.

> 1 bunch fresh dandelion greens
> 1 red onion
> 1 cup grape tomatoes
> ¼ cup packed fresh basil leaves
> 3 tablespoons white balsamic vinegar
> 3 tablespoons flax oil
> 3 tablespoons extra-virgin olive oil
> 4 cloves peeled garlic
> 1 teaspoon Dijon mustard
> ¼ teaspoon sea salt
> ¼ teaspoon freshly ground black pepper

Slice the dandelion greens across the grain at intervals of 1½ to 2 inches. Refresh and crisp the cut greens in a large bowl of cold water for about 5 minutes. Drain well. Dry the greens in a salad spinner or roll them gently in a towel to absorb the excess water. Transfer to a dry bowl.

Cut the onion in half lengthwise, and then slice it thinly across the grain. Add the onion to the greens in the bowl.

Wash and dry the grape tomatoes but keep them in a small bowl or on a plate until serving time.

Put the basil, vinegar, flax oil, olive oil, garlic, mustard, salt, and pepper in a blender. Process for 45 to 60 seconds, or until smooth. Pour over the salad and toss thoroughly. Divide the salad among 4 plates. Top each serving with the tomatoes. Serve at once.

Per serving: calories: 255, protein: 3 g, fat: 21 g, carbohydrate: 13 g, fiber: 3 g, sodium: 207 mg, omega-3 fatty acids: 5.4 g

CUCUMBERS IN TARATOUR SAUCE

Makes 4 servings

Taratour, perhaps best known as a sauce served with falafel, is basically a thin hummus without the garbanzo beans. Since cucumbers are a staple in Middle Eastern cuisine, it came to me that this sauce would taste great with them. Something about the rich, creamy sesame against the refreshing crunch of cucumber gets your mouth going in two directions in a way that really works. Try Taratour Sauce with other vegetables, like raw or lightly steamed cauliflower and broccoli.

1 English cucumber
4 cloves peeled garlic, coarsely chopped
½ teaspoons salt
2 tablespoons tahini
2 to 3 tablespoons freshly squeezed lemon juice
2 tablespoons extra-virgin olive oil
1 tablespoon plus 1 teaspoon finely chopped fresh parsley

Peel the cucumber, quarter it lengthwise, and then cut it into ½-inch chunks. Transfer the cucumber to a bowl.

Pound the garlic in a mortar with the salt until velvety smooth and creamy. Combine the tahini, 2 tablespoons of the lemon juice, and all of the oil in a small bowl. Stir until well blended. Stir in the mashed garlic and salt. Add 1 tablespoon of the parsley and stir well. Taste and add more lemon juice, if needed.

Pour the sauce over the cucumbers and toss well. Serve in small bowls, garnished with the remaining teaspoon of parsley.

Per serving: calories: 132, protein: 3 g, fat: 11 g, carbohydrate: 8 g, fiber: 2 g, sodium: 276 mg, omega-3 fatty acids: 0.05 g

EATING SHOOTS AND LEAVES

Makes 4 servings

After my first tête-à-tête with an editor, I realized how much I didn't know about writing in my own native tongue. Among several books I subsequently picked up on the subtle art of punctuation, *Eats, Shoots & Leaves* by Lynne Truss had the most intriguing, and memorable, title. Eating shoots and leaves here—and sprouts—well, I just couldn't resist.

1 bunch watercress
8 ounces mung bean sprouts
3 ounces pea shoots
1 bunch scallions, sliced
1 (¾-inch-thick) slice fresh pineapple, cut into ¼-inch dice
1 roasted red pepper, cut into ¼-inch dice
½ cup roasted cashews (salted or unsalted, as you prefer)
⅓ cup walnut oil
3 tablespoons brown rice vinegar
2 tablespoons freshly squeezed lime juice
2 tablespoons minced fresh lemongrass
1 tablespoon minced fresh ginger
2 teaspoons palm sugar
3 cloves peeled garlic
1 teaspoon Sriracha sauce
½ teaspoon sea salt
¼ teaspoon freshly ground black pepper

Combine the watercress, bean sprouts, pea shoots, scallions, pineapple, red pepper, and cashews in a large bowl.

Put the oil, vinegar, lime juice, lemongrass, ginger, palm sugar, garlic, Sriracha sauce, salt, and pepper in a blender. Process until smooth, stopping to scrape down the sides of the blender jar as needed. Pour over the vegetables and toss thoroughly. Divide among 4 plates. Serve at once.

Per serving: calories: 319, protein: 6 g, fat: 26 g, carbohydrate: 15 g, fiber: 3 g, sodium: 351 mg, omega-3 fatty acids: 0 g

GLASS NOODLE SALAD WITH SPICY PEANUT SAUCE

Makes 4 servings

I've never been a fan of pasta salads, but this one is a notable exception. It's oddly cooling on a hot summer day, despite the initial heat from the sauce. "Glass noodles" is the poetic name for mung bean threads (also known as saifun, which is the most common name on labels). These are vermicelli-like Chinese noodles that become translucent when cooked. The sauce can be thinned with a little water and used with other kinds of noodles, such as brown rice spaghetti or buckwheat soba. Simply omit the cucumbers and stir the sauce into the pasta as soon as it is cooked, for a warm *and* spicy dish. The sauce can also be used on other salads. It keeps well, so if you like it, next time make a double quantity and keep the unused portion in the refrigerator.

8 ounces saifun (mung bean threads)
1 tablespoon toasted sesame oil
2 English cucumbers
1 cup coarsely chopped fresh cilantro
1/4 cup tamari
2 tablespoons Sriracha sauce
2 tablespoons agave nectar
1 tablespoon chopped garlic
1 tablespoon chopped fresh ginger
1 tablespoon dry sherry
1/4 cup peanut butter
2 tablespoons sesame seeds

Place the saifun noodles in a large, heatproof bowl. Cover the noodles with boiling water and let soak for about 5 minutes, stirring from time to time with a pair of chopsticks. Once the noodles are tender (give them the bite test), drain and rinse with cold water, and then drain again thoroughly. Transfer to a bowl. Sprinkle with 2 teaspoons of the sesame oil and toss gently.

Cut the cucumbers on a diagonal into 1/4-inch-thick slices. Stack a few of the slices at a time and cut them lengthwise into 1/4-inch-thick sticks. Add the sticks to the noodles.

To make the sauce, put ½ cup of the cilantro, the remaining teaspoon of sesame oil, and all of the tamari, Sriracha sauce, agave nectar, garlic, ginger, and sherry in a blender. Process until smooth. With the motor running, add the peanut butter, a spoonful at a time, through the cap opening in the lid, blending until smooth. Make sure the consistency is not too thick or too runny. If it is too thick, add a little vegetable broth or water.

Pour the sauce over the noodles and cucumbers. Add 1 teaspoon of the sesame seeds and ¼ cup of the remaining cilantro. Toss well. Divide among 4 plates. Top with the remaining ¼ cup of cilantro. Serve at once.

Per serving: calories: 455, protein: 9 g, fat: 13 g, carbohydrate: 75 g, fiber: 4 g, sodium: 1,341 mg, omega-3 fatty acids: 0 g

FENNEL SLAW

Makes 4 servings

Fennel is an appetite enhancer, a digestive aid, and a palate cleanser, but most importantly, it's freaking delicious. This salad is good at the beginning of a meal, at the end of a meal, or by itself as a snack. To keep the fennel from discoloring, make the dressing first, and then cut the fennel.

    3 tablespoons white balsamic vinegar
    1 teaspoon Dijon mustard
    ½ teaspoon sea salt
    ¼ teaspoon freshly ground black pepper
    ¼ cup flax oil
    4 medium-size fennel bulbs
    1 red onion
    ¼ cup lightly chopped fennel fronds

To make the dressing, whisk the vinegar, mustard, salt, and pepper in a small bowl. Continue whisking while slowly adding the oil in a thin stream. Once the dressing has emulsified, set it aside.

If the fennel is very fresh, the surface will be smooth and appetizing; if not, use a peeler to strip off the discolored outer layer. Slice the fennel bulbs in half lengthwise and cut out the tough core. Slice it thinly across the grain.

Cut the onion into quarters lengthwise; then slice it thinly across the grain. Combine the fennel, onion, and fennel fronds in a medium bowl. Whisk the dressing once more to emulsify it again, if necessary. Pour the dressing over the vegetables. Toss well. Serve at once.

Per serving: calories: 178, protein: 2 g, fat: 13 g, carbohydrate: 9 g, fiber: 4 g, sodium: 359 mg, omega-3 fatty acids: 7 g

GRAPE TOMATO AND GARBANZO SALAD

Makes 4 servings

You'll need very small tomatoes for this salad, preferably no more than twice the size of the garbanzos. This is for more than mere visual effect—it's all about the sensation of little tomatoes exploding and blending suddenly with the other flavors in your mouth. If you can find frozen green garbanzos, by all means substitute them for the canned ones—they are far superior for this application. You'll just need to blanch them for a few minutes in boiling salted water, rinse them in cold water, and drain well before proceeding. It's well worth the effort.

> 2 cups cooked or canned garbanzo beans, rinsed and drained
> 7 ounces tiny, ripe grape tomatoes (about 1½ cups)
> 1 cup finely diced red onion
> ½ cup coarsely chopped fresh basil
> 6 tablespoons Balsamic Vinaigrette (page 44)
> 1 tablespoon finely chopped fresh Italian parsley
> Lettuce (optional)

Combine the beans, tomatoes, onion, basil, vinaigrette, and parsley in a medium bowl. Toss thoroughly. Serve at once, in small bowls or on a bed of lettuce.

Per serving: calories: 295, protein: 8 g, fat: 16 g, carbohydrate: 23 g, fiber: 8 g, sodium: 197 mg, omega-3 fatty acids: 3.6 g

GREEN BEAN AND GARBANZO SALAD

Makes 4 servings

Bright green and deliciously pungent, this salad makes a satisfying light lunch as well as an effective appetizer for a larger meal. Thai green curry paste, which provides an exotic background note and fires up the heat nicely, is the base for the dressing. If you are unable to find frozen green garbanzos, shelled edamame are the ideal substitute.

> 2 teaspoons sea salt
> 2 cups frozen cut green beans
> 3 cups frozen green garbanzo beans or frozen shelled edamame
> 2 bunches scallions, sliced on a diagonal
> 1 avocado, cut into ¼-inch dice
> 1 large bunch fresh cilantro
> ¼ cup freshly squeezed lime juice
> ¼ cup flax or extra-virgin olive oil
> 2 tablespoons white balsamic vinegar
> 1 tablespoon Thai green curry paste
> Watercress (optional)

Fill a large pot with water and 1 teaspoon of the salt. Bring to a boil. Add the green beans and cook until just tender-crisp, about 1 minute. Keeping the water boiling, scoop the beans out with a slotted spoon or Chinese strainer. Refresh them under cold running water and drain thoroughly. Transfer to a medium bowl.

Add the garbanzo beans to the boiling water, stirring well. Cook for about 2 minutes, or until the beans are just tender but still retain a little bite. Drain, refresh under cold running water, and drain again thoroughly. Transfer to the bowl with the green beans, along with the scallions and avocado.

Wash the cilantro and separate the leaves from the stems. Coarsely chop the leaves and add them to the bean mixture. Put the stems in a blender along with the lime juice, oil, vinegar, and curry paste. Process until smooth. Pour over the bean mixture and toss very gently to avoid mashing the avocado. Serve at once, in small bowls or on a bed of watercress.

Per serving: calories: 461, protein: 21 g, fat: 30 g, carbohydrate: 20 g, fiber: 13 g, sodium: 632 mg, omega-3 fatty acids: 7.1 g

GREEN CURRY SALAD

Makes 4 servings

With its bright tastes and crunchy textures, this salad is a crowd-pleaser. Just beware: it has to be eaten right away, so whatever you do, don't add the dressing until just before you're ready to serve it. If watercress isn't available, substitute with Chinese cabbage, mustard greens, Tuscan kale, tat soi, mizuna, baby bok choy, or any combination of these.

1½ cups thinly sliced green or savoy cabbage
1 bunch watercress
8 ounces mung bean sprouts
3 stalks celery, thinly sliced on a diagonal
1 carrot, grated
1 lime
½ cup packed fresh basil leaves
5 tablespoons brown rice vinegar
4 tablespoons flax oil
4 cloves peeled garlic
1 tablespoon Thai green curry paste
1 teaspoon sea salt
½ cup toasted cashews, lightly crushed

Combine the cabbage, watercress, bean sprouts, celery, and carrot in a large bowl.

Carefully peel the zest from the lime with a vegetable peeler as thinly as possible and put it in a blender. Squeeze the lime juice into the blender. Add the basil, vinegar, oil, garlic, curry paste, and salt. Process for about 1 minute, or until smooth. Pour over the vegetables in the bowl. Toss thoroughly. Divide among 4 plates. Top with the cashews. Serve at once.

Per serving: calories: 280, protein: 6 g, fat: 22 g, carbohydrate: 13 g, fiber: 3 g, sodium: 655 mg, omega-3 fatty acids: 7.1 g

Facing this page: Hot Eggplant and Seitan Open-Face Sandwich, 54–55
Following page: Papadums with Fresh Green Chutney, 52–53; Tempeh Sticks with Peanut Sauce, 56

ICEBERG WEDGES WITH ESSENTIAL FATTY ACID DRESSING

Makes 4 servings

Blanching garlic smoothes some of its pungent edge, enabling a creamy, less intense but still good and garlicky dressing. Feel free to add other salad items, but I think this dish is iconic with simple, crunchy iceberg lettuce. Your call.

½ cup peeled garlic cloves
½ cup flax oil
4 tablespoons freshly squeezed lemon juice
½ teaspoon sea salt
¼ teaspoon freshly ground black pepper
1 large or 2 small heads iceberg lettuce

To make the dressing, drop the garlic cloves into a small pot of boiling water, decrease the heat, and simmer gently for 15 minutes. Drain, refresh under cold water, and drain again thoroughly. Transfer to a blender. Add the oil, lemon juice, salt, and pepper. Process until smooth.

Remove and discard any bruised or wilted outer leaves from the lettuce, and then cut it into small wedges. Arrange on 4 plates. Pour the dressing evenly over the lettuce. Serve at once.

Tip: Alternatively, cut the lettuce into bite-size cubes. Transfer to a large bowl. Add the dressing, and then toss until evenly coated.

Per serving: calories: 309, protein: 3 g, fat: 26 g, carbohydrate: 14 g, fiber: 1 g, sodium: 280 mg, omega-3 fatty acids: 14.2 g

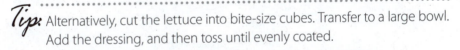

Previous page: Leek and Cauliflower Soup, 62–63; Pimento Soup with Vermouth, 58–59
Facing this page: Campari-Braised Radicchio Salad with Grapefruit, 108–109

GRILLED VEGETABLE SALAD WITH SPICY MISO

Makes 4 to 6 servings

Grilled vegetables almost don't need any further treatment to be delicious, but this light miso dressing provides an unusual envelope of flavors that pulls everything together exquisitely. Sort of an East-meets-Mediterranean salad. Don't let the number of ingredients scare you away—this is a lot easier and faster to make than it may seem.

- 1 eggplant, cut lengthwise into ½-inch-thick slices
- 4 small zucchini, cut lengthwise into ¼-inch-thick slices
- 1 red onion, cut into ½-inch-thick slices
- 2 portobello mushrooms, stems removed
- 2 roasted red peppers, quartered
- 2 roasted yellow peppers, quartered (optional)
- ¼ cup extra-virgin olive oil
- ½ teaspoon sea salt
- ½ teaspoon freshly ground black pepper
- 3 tablespoons mellow white miso
- 2 tablespoons flax oil
- Grated zest of 1 lemon
- 2 tablespoons freshly squeezed lemon juice
- 1 tablespoon agave nectar
- 1 teaspoon tamari
- 1 clove peeled garlic, pressed
- ¼ teaspoon Sriracha sauce
- 2 tablespoons chopped fresh parsley

Preheat a grill (outdoor or stovetop).

Brush the eggplant, zucchini, onion, mushrooms, and roasted peppers very lightly with the olive oil. Season the vegetables with the salt and pepper and place them on the grill. Cook for about 2 minutes on each side, or until tender but not mushy. Transfer to a platter and let cool slightly.

While the vegetables are cooking, prepare the dressing. Combine the miso, flax oil, lemon zest, lemon juice, agave nectar, tamari, garlic, and Sriracha sauce in a large bowl. Whisk until well blended.

When the vegetables are cool enough to handle, cut them into bite-size pieces and add them to the bowl of dressing along with 1 tablespoon of the parsley. Toss gently but thoroughly. Serve at once, garnished with a sprinkling of the remaining tablespoon of parsley.

Per serving: calories: 233, protein: 4 g, fat: 17 g, carbohydrate: 14 g, fiber: 5 g, sodium: 537 mg, omega-3 fatty acids: 3 g

GREEN SALAD WITH ASPARAGUS AND SHIITAKE MUSHROOMS

Makes 4 servings

This salad can be made with any combination of mixed lettuces, but the miso-based dressing goes especially well with Asian greens. Look for tender young asparagus, as thin as possible, for the best results. Make sure you use very fresh walnut oil—the slightest rancidity will ruin the whole dish. If you can't find any good walnut oil, it would be preferable to use almond oil or even extra-virgin olive oil (in spite of its strong taste).

    3 tablespoons walnut oil
    2 tablespoons mellow white miso
    2 tablespoons brown rice vinegar
    1 tablespoon mirin
    1 tablespoon tamari
    1 teaspoon toasted sesame oil
    4 ounces tender young asparagus, cut into 2-inch lengths
    1 roasted red pepper
    8 ounces mixed Asian greens
    6 fresh shiitake mushrooms, thinly sliced
    ½ cup thinly sliced celery hearts, leaves included
    ½ cup sliced water chestnuts (preferably fresh)
    ¼ cup thinly sliced shallots
    1 tablespoon sesame seeds

Combine the walnut oil, miso, vinegar, mirin, tamari, and sesame oil in a small bowl. Whisk until smooth.

Blanch the asparagus in boiling salted water for 15 seconds. Immediately drain and plunge into ice water to stop the cooking. Remove from the water and place on a towel to drain thoroughly.

Quarter the red pepper, and then cut it crosswise into ⅛-inch-thick slices.

Place the greens in a large bowl. Add the asparagus, red pepper, mushrooms, celery, water chestnuts, shallots, and sesame seeds. Toss well. Serve at once.

Per serving: calories: 196, protein: 4 g, fat: 13 g, carbohydrate: 13 g, fiber: 4 g, sodium: 538 mg, omega-3 fatty acids: 0 g

HOMINY AND BLACK BEAN SALAD

Makes 8 to 10 servings

This salad makes a good buffet item for potlucks. Hominy is corn that has been dried and then cooked in limewater until the outer skin falls off, a process that softens the corn and makes it more digestible. It also boosts the calcium content. Known in Mexico as *nixtamal*, hominy is also ground to a thick paste and used to make a number of traditional corn cakes, including tortillas, tamales, sopes, and gorditas (none of which fit the thirty-minute window allowed here, especially for a beginner!).

> 1 can (29 ounces) hominy, well drained
> 1 can (15 ounces) black beans, rinsed and drained
> 2 stalks celery, diced
> 1 green bell pepper, diced
> 1 roasted red pepper, diced
> 1 red onion, finely diced
> 1 avocado, diced
> 1½ cups coarsely chopped fresh cilantro
> ½ cup freshly squeezed lime juice
> 7 cloves peeled garlic
> 2 teaspoons Chipotle Chile Purée (page 40)
> 1 teaspoon sea salt
> ½ teaspoon freshly ground black pepper
> ¾ cup extra-virgin olive oil
> 1 bunch scallions, sliced on a diagonal

Combine the hominy, black beans, celery, green bell pepper, red pepper, onion, avocado, and 1 cup of the cilantro in a large bowl.

Put the remaining ½ cup of cilantro and all of the lime juice, garlic, Chipotle Chile Purée, salt, and pepper in a blender. Process until smooth. With the motor running, add the olive oil in a steady stream through the cap opening in the lid. Pour over the hominy mixture and toss well. Transfer to a large serving dish. Sprinkle with the scallions. Serve at once.

Per serving: calories: 338, protein: 6 g, fat: 23 g, carbohydrate: 21 g, fiber: 9 g, sodium: 452 mg, omega-3 fatty acids: 0.13 g

MEXISRAELI SALAD

Makes 4 to 6 servings

Combining Mexican flavors with a traditional Israeli salad makes for an interesting variation, especially if you like spicy food and include the chiles and Chipotle Chile Purée. In Mexico City, where I grew up, there were a lot of Jewish expats from all over Europe, most of whom blended right in, so this actually wasn't much of a stretch, from my perspective.

16 to 18 large cherry tomatoes
1 English cucumber
1 can (25 ounces) garbanzo beans, rinsed and drained
2 avocados, cut into ½-inch dice
1 red onion, finely diced
1 green bell pepper, cut into ½-inch dice
1 cup coarsely chopped fresh cilantro
1 or 2 fresh green serrano chiles (optional)
⅓ cup freshly squeezed lime juice
¼ cup extra-virgin olive oil
2 tablespoons flax oil
1 teaspoon Chipotle Chile Purée (page 40; optional)
½ teaspoon sea salt
½ teaspoon freshly ground black pepper

Cut the cherry tomatoes in half. Put them in a large bowl.

Peel the cucumber. Quarter it lengthwise, and then cut it crosswise into ½-inch-thick slices. Add to the bowl with the tomatoes. Add the garbanzo beans, avocado, onion, bell pepper, cilantro, and chiles, if using.

To make the dressing, combine the lime juice, olive oil, flax oil, Chipotle Chile Purée, if using, salt, and pepper in a separate bowl. Whisk until emulsified. Add to the vegetable mixture. Toss gently but thoroughly. Serve at once.

Tip: To make this dish a few hours in advance, prepare all the vegetables, except for the avocado, and put in a bowl with the garbanzo beans. Cover and refrigerate. Prepare the dressing in a separate bowl. Add the diced avocado and toss gently to coat. (This will prevent the avocado from discoloring.) Cover and refrigerate. Just before serving, add the dressing and avocado to the vegetable mixture. Serve at once.

Per serving: calories: 445, protein: 11 g, fat: 30 g, carbohydrate: 29 g, fiber: 13 g, sodium: 238 mg, omega-3 fatty acids: 2.92 g

ISRAELI SALAD

Makes 4 to 6 servings

The addition of garbanzo beans to a traditional Israeli salad might be unortho-dox, but they go very well with it and provide an excellent source of protein. Call it a "Reform Jewish salad," if that feels right to you. Salt will draw out the liquid in the cucumber, softening it and making the mixture soupy, so be sure to add the salt just at the last minute.

> 16 large cherry tomatoes
> 1 English cucumber
> 1 can (25 ounces) garbanzo beans, rinsed and drained
> 1 red onion, finely diced
> 1 green bell pepper, cut into 1/2-inch dice
> 1/2 cup coarsely chopped fresh parsley
> 1/3 cup extra-virgin olive oil
> 1/4 cup freshly squeezed lemon juice
> 1/2 teaspoon sea salt
> 1/2 teaspoon freshly ground black pepper

Cut the cherry tomatoes in half. Put them in a large bowl.

Peel the cucumber. Quarter it lengthwise, and then cut it crosswise into 1/2-inch-thick slices. Add to the bowl with the tomatoes.

Add the garbanzo beans, onion, bell pepper, parsley, olive oil, and lemon juice. Toss well. Just before serving, add the salt and pepper and toss again.

Per serving: calories: 270, protein: 8 g, fat: 15 g, carbohydrate: 26 g, fiber: 6 g, sodium: 236 mg, omega-3 fatty acids: 0.1 g

JICAMA SALAD WITH AVOCADO-LIME DRESSING

Makes 4 servings

Very crisp and succulent, with a rich, creamy dressing, this is a perfect summer salad. In Mexico, jicama is a classic street food, usually served sliced or in sticks, sprinkled with fresh lime juice, red chile powder, and salt. When selecting the jicama, look for smooth, unblemished skin, and flesh that is very firm to the touch. Good jicama has the interesting feature of being dry and juicy at the same time. Like a mealy peach, one bad jicama can turn people off to a good thing forever.

1 large jicama
½ head iceberg lettuce
2 ripe avocados
¼ cup freshly squeezed lime juice
¼ cup flax oil
½ teaspoon sea salt
¼ teaspoon freshly ground black pepper
2 limes, segmented and cut into small pieces
¼ cup chopped shallot
1½ tablespoons chopped fresh tarragon

Peel the jicama. Slice it a little thicker than ¼ inch. Stack the slices, and then cut them into sticks about 2 inches long and ¼ inch thick.

Cut the lettuce into 1-inch cubes.

Cut 1 of the avocados into ¼-inch dice and set aside.

To make the dressing, put the remaining avocado and the lime juice in a blender. Process until smooth. With the motor running, add the oil, salt, and pepper through the cap opening in the lid. Pour into a large bowl.

Gently fold the reserved avocado, lime segments, shallot, and tarragon into the dressing. Add the jicama sticks and lettuce cubes. Toss gently to coat. Serve at once.

Per serving: calories: 348, protein: 5 g, fat: 28 g, carbohydrate: 14 g, fiber: 13 g, sodium: 276 mg, omega-3 fatty acids: 7.1 g

MOROCCANESQUE CARROT SALAD

Makes 4 servings

The traditional Moroccan salad is made with honey, but I find there is no mortal insult to the dish by substituting agave nectar (except culturally, but we're in a global economy now, so who really cares that much?). I've also mucked with it by cutting the olive oil 50/50 with flax oil. Moroccans are tolerant, so I'm fairly certain there will be no hard feelings. Served in a large lettuce leaf, this is a mouthwatering appetizer.

1 pound carrots, peeled and coarsely grated
⅓ cup currants
3 tablespoons extra-virgin olive oil
3 tablespoons flax oil
2 tablespoons freshly squeezed lemon juice
1 tablespoon dark agave nectar
1 teaspoon ground cinnamon, plus more for garnish
½ teaspoon sea salt
¼ teaspoon freshly ground black pepper
3 tablespoons slivered almonds, lightly toasted

Put the carrots and currants in a large bowl.

Combine the olive oil, flax oil, lemon juice, agave nectar, cinnamon, salt, and pepper in a small bowl. Whisk until emulsified. Pour over the carrots and currants and toss until evenly distributed. Let sit for at about 15 minutes to allow the flavors to develop.

Toss again just before serving. Garnish with the almonds and a light sprinkling of cinnamon.

Per serving: calories: 315, protein: 3 g, fat: 24 g, carbohydrate: 21 g, fiber: 5 g, sodium: 346 mg, omega-3 fatty acids: 5.4 g

POTATO SALAD WITH SALSA VERDE

Makes 6 to 8 servings

Salsa verde is an Italian sauce normally served with steamed or grilled fish, but I find that it excels as a foil for potatoes. In this version, I solved the quandary of what to do with beet tops, in case that ever troubled you. You can serve this salad hot or cold with equal delight.

3 pounds new potatoes
4 cups fresh beet greens (tops)
1 tablespoon plus 1 teaspoon sea salt
¼ cup extra-virgin olive oil
¼ cup flax oil
2 tablespoons capers
2 tablespoons chopped fresh parsley
1 tablespoon freshly squeezed lemon juice
4 cloves peeled garlic, minced or pressed
1 teaspoon Dijon mustard
½ teaspoon freshly ground black pepper

Bring a large pot of water to a boil.

Cut the potatoes into bite-size pieces or in half, if they are small, so they will absorb the flavor of the sauce.

Wash the beet greens well to remove any grit. When the water is boiling, drop in the greens and stir for about 1 minute. Scoop out the greens with a slotted spoon and put them in a colander in the sink. Rinse the greens under cold running water. Squeeze all the water out of the greens and set aside.

When the water returns to a boil, add the potatoes and 1 tablespoon of the salt. Return to a boil, cover, and cook for 15 to 20 minutes, until the potatoes are just tender.

While the potatoes are cooking, put the beet greens in the work bowl of a food processor. Add the olive oil, flax oil, capers, parsley, lemon juice, garlic, mustard, pepper, and the remaining teaspoon of salt. Pulse until the mixture is finely chopped and well mixed. Scrape into a large bowl.

As soon as the potatoes are done, drain them in a colander, shaking gently to allow all the water to drip out. Immediately transfer the potatoes to the bowl with the beet green mixture. Toss well. Serve at once, or let cool and then refrigerate until cold.

Per serving: calories: 314, protein: 5 g, fat: 16 g, carbohydrate: 40 g, fiber: 4 g, sodium: 456 mg, omega-3 fatty acids: 4.11 g

NAPA SLAW

Makes 4 to 6 servings

Nothing compares with fresh, raw vegetables, especially dressed with vibrant Asian flavors. Something about this mouthwatering combination is downright thrilling to the palate. Served in smaller portions, this slaw makes a stimulating appetizer as part of a multicourse meal. It should be eaten right away; but even wilted the following day, it still retains a lot of its original appeal.

    4 cups thinly sliced napa cabbage (about ½ head)
    2 carrots, grated
    2 stalks celery, thinly sliced on a diagonal
    1 fennel bulb, thinly sliced (optional)
    1 red bell pepper, cut into thin strips
    1 bunch scallions, thinly sliced on a diagonal
    ½ cup coarsely chopped fresh cilantro
    ⅓ cup hempseeds
    1 tablespoon sesame seeds
    ¼ cup freshly squeezed lime juice
    2 tablespoons tahini
    1 tablespoon mirin
    1 tablespoon tamari
    1 tablespoon agave nectar
    1 teaspoon toasted sesame oil
    1 teaspoon Sriracha sauce

Combine the cabbage, carrots, celery, fennel, if using, red bell pepper, scallions, cilantro, hempseeds, and sesame seeds in a large bowl.

Combine the lime juice, tahini, mirin, tamari, agave nectar, sesame oil, and Sriracha sauce in a small bowl. Whisk until emulsified. Pour over the vegetable mixture and toss thoroughly to coat. Serve at once.

Per serving: calories: 193, protein: 9 g, fat: 10 g, carbohydrate: 15 g, fiber: 5 g, sodium: 304 mg, omega-3 fatty acids: 1 g

MISO—RED CURRY SLAW

Makes 4 to 6 servings　　　　　　　　(See photo facing page 134.)

This is a bright and spicy dish to serve on its own or as an appetizer. I originally made it with Panang curry paste (which makes my eyes roll back in ecstasy), but I later discovered that this mixture features dried shrimp paste (curses!). If you're industrious and die-hard dedicated enough to hand-pound your own Panang curry paste from fresh ingredients *without* shrimp paste, I highly recommend this in place of the commercial red curry paste, as it is truly incomparable. If not, rest assured the result will still amaze one and all. Consider adding any of your favorite slaw ingredients, such as green cabbage, napa cabbage, grated beets, or others. The primary goal is to enjoy a spicy, richly flavored, crunchy, raw delight. Feel free to use whichever nuts and nut butter you wish. I like macadamia nuts for their mild, buttery crunch, with cashew-macadamia butter as a complement in the dressing, but almost any nut will work well in this salad, especially tropical nuts.

- 2 green bell peppers
- 5 tablespoons freshly squeezed lime juice
- 2 tablespoons mellow white miso
- 1 tablespoon Thai red curry paste
- 1 tablespoon peeled and chopped fresh ginger
- 4 cloves peeled garlic
- ½ teaspoon sea salt
- 4 tablespoons cashew-macadamia nut butter, cashew butter, almond butter, or tahini
- ⅓ cup almond, flax, or extra-virgin olive oil
- 4 cups shredded red cabbage
- 2 cups shredded carrots
- 2 cups mung bean sprouts
- 2 bunches scallions, sliced on a diagonal
- ½ cup chopped fresh basil
- ½ cup chopped fresh cilantro
- ½ cup coarsely chopped macadamia nuts or cashews

Preheat the broiler.

Quarter the bell peppers and remove the seeds and membranes. Lay the pieces skin-side up on a baking sheet and place under the broiler for about 5 minutes, until the skin begins to blister and blacken. Immediately immerse in cold water. The skins should slip off easily, but if any parts are stubborn, scrape them off with a knife. Slice the pepper pieces about ¼ inch thick and set aside.

To make the dressing, put the lime juice, miso, curry paste, ginger, garlic, and salt in a blender. Process until smooth. With the motor running, add the nut butter through the cap opening in the lid, followed by the oil.

Combine the cabbage, carrots, bean sprouts, and peppers in a large bowl. Add the dressing and toss well. Add the scallions, basil, cilantro, and macadamia nuts. Toss until evenly distributed. Serve at once.

Per serving: calories: 381, protein: 8 g, fat: 31 g, carbohydrate: 19 g, fiber: 6 g, sodium: 532 mg, omega-3 fatty acids: 0 g

QUICK BEET SLAW

Makes 4 servings

Not only is this fast and easy, but it also travels well, making it an ideal picnic food. Be sure to take something to stir it with before serving, though, because the vegetables will drain a bit, and you'll want to redistribute the juices well.

1 medium-size beet, scrubbed or peeled and grated
1 carrot, grated
1 roasted red pepper, quartered and cut crosswise into ¼-inch-thick slices
½ red onion, quartered and thinly sliced
½ cup coarsely chopped fresh cilantro
½ cup coarsely chopped fresh basil
2 stalks celery, thinly sliced
2 radishes, grated
½ cup flax oil
2 tablespoons brown rice vinegar
Grated zest of 1 lime
2 tablespoons freshly squeezed lime juice
4 cloves peeled garlic
2 teaspoons Dijon mustard
½ teaspoon sea salt
½ teaspoon freshly ground black pepper

Combine the beets, carrots, red pepper, and onion in a large bowl. Add ¼ cup of the cilantro, ¼ cup of the basil, and all of the celery and radishes.

Put the flax oil, vinegar, lime zest, lime juice, garlic, mustard, salt, and pepper in a blender. Process until smooth. Pour over the vegetable mixture. Toss well. Eat.

Per serving: calories: 287, protein: 1 g, fat: 27 g, carbohydrate: 7 g, fiber: 2 g, sodium: 379 mg, omega-3 fatty acids: 14.2 g

RADISH AND BLACK BEAN SALAD

Makes 4 to 6 servings

Black beans are a miraculous food, highly regarded for both their flavor and healthful properties in a number of cuisines, including macrobiotics (which shuns green pepper as a member of the deadly nightshade family, which is one reason I wasn't able to stay in the macro fold). This salad was inspired by a radish relish served in Veracruz, on the Mexican Gulf Coast. No beans in that recipe, but I bet they just never thought of it.

1 can (15 ounces) black beans, rinsed and drained
1½ cups diced green bell pepper
1 cup diced radishes
1 cup finely diced red onion
1 cup diced celery hearts, with leaves
¼ cup flax oil
2 tablespoons freshly squeezed lime juice
2 tablespoons brown rice vinegar
1 tablespoon tamari
4 cloves peeled garlic, minced or pressed
1 teaspoon Chipotle Chile Purée (page 40)
½ teaspoon sea salt
¼ teaspoon freshly ground black pepper

Combine the beans, bell pepper, radishes, onion, and celery in a large bowl.
Combine the flax oil, lime juice, vinegar, tamari, garlic, Chipotle Chile Purée, salt, and pepper in a small bowl. Whisk until emulsified. Pour over the vegetable mixture. Toss until thoroughly coated. Serve at once.

Per serving: calories: 247, protein: 9 g, fat: 12 g, carbohydrate: 19 g, fiber: 9 g, sodium: 430 mg, omega-3 fatty acids: 5.68 g

SALAD OF FENNEL, ROASTED PEPPERS, AND ROMAINE HEARTS

Makes 4 to 6 servings

The combination of very crisp fennel and lettuce with yielding roasted peppers, bound by a mild, emerald green fennel vinaigrette, is a showstopper. If you can't find a jar of roasted yellow peppers, substitute with additional red ones (which are everywhere). This is an ideal salad to end a rich meal, as it both cleanses and delights the palate. You could even get away with not offering a dessert after this. Maybe.

        2 bulbs fennel
        1 romaine heart (inner leaves only)
        1 red onion
        2 roasted red peppers
        1 roasted yellow pepper
        1 cup Fennel Vinaigrette (page 69)

If the fennel has any discoloration or bruising, first pare away the dry outer skin with a vegetable peeler (this is preferable to removing the entire outer layers). Cut each bulb in half lengthwise and cut out the core. Slice it crosswise, a little under 1/8 inch thick. Drop the slices into a large bowl of cold water.

Cut the romaine leaves in half lengthwise, and then slice them crosswise into pieces 2 to 2 1/2 inches long. Add the lettuce to the fennel and let them soak while you prepare the rest of the ingredients. This will crisp the vegetables and at the same time prevent the fennel from oxidizing.

Cut the onion in half lengthwise, and then slice it thinly crosswise. Break up the slices into a large bowl.

Slice the peppers into strips. Add them to the bowl with the onion.

Drain the lettuce and fennel. Dry it in a salad spinner or roll it gently in a towel to absorb the excess water. Add to the peppers and onion.

Pour about half of the vinaigrette over the vegetables and toss well. Taste and add more vinaigrette, if needed. Toss again. Serve at once.

Per serving: calories: 258, protein: 2 g, fat: 22 g, carbohydrate: 11 g, fiber: 3 g, sodium: 296 mg, omega-3 fatty acids: 0.16 g

"SMOKED" PORTOBELLO MUSHROOM SALAD

Makes about 4 servings

This is perfect as a warm salad, freshly tossed with the mushrooms right out of the oven, but it is just as delectable at room temperature or cold. The smoky flavor is imparted by two ingredients: smoked salt and smoked paprika. They may take a little effort to find, but the effect is well worth the trouble. Also, you'll have plenty left over to use in other dishes, and you'll want to, believe me. I recommend buying them from online sources, which will save you a bundle over fancy gourmet shops.

> 4 large portobello mushroom caps
> 1/4 cup extra-virgin olive oil
> 1 1/2 teaspoons smoked salt
> 1 teaspoon smoked paprika
> 1/2 teaspoon freshly ground black pepper
> 1/2 cup finely diced shallots
> 1/4 cup chopped fresh parsley
> 4 teaspoons balsamic vinegar

Preheat the oven to 425 degrees F. Line 2 baking sheets with parchment paper.

Wash the mushrooms and pat them dry with towels. Using a very sharp knife (to avoid breaking them), cut the mushrooms into 1/4-inch-thick slices. Arrange the slices, cut-side up, in a single layer on the prepared baking sheets and rub them with a light coating of the olive oil. Combine the smoked salt, smoked paprika, and pepper in a small bowl. Dust the mushrooms evenly with the mixture. The easiest way to do this is to put the mixture in a salt shaker with holes large enough to allow the pepper to pass through. Bake the mushrooms for 10 minutes.

While the mushrooms are baking, combine the shallots, parsley, and vinegar in a medium bowl. As soon as the mushrooms are done, remove them from the oven and slide them off the parchment paper, along with any accumulated juices, directly into the bowl. Toss well. Serve at once.

Per serving: calories: 155, protein: 3 g, fat: 14 g, carbohydrate: 6 g, fiber: 1 g, sodium: 809 mg, omega-3 fatty acids: 0.1 g

SPICY CUCUMBER SALAD

Makes 4 servings

Japanese cucumbers are very thin, about half the thickness of English cucumbers. If you have trouble locating them, substitute with pickling cucumbers—not as delicate, but close enough. To be honest, this salad doesn't need any oil. It's one of many Asian pickled salads that typically are all salt and vinegar. However, the small amount of flax oil doesn't hurt it any, and it does a body good, so why not? Hey—it works!

    4 Japanese cucumbers, or 6 pickling cucumbers
    2 teaspoons sea salt
    1 teaspoon crushed red chile flakes
    1 clove peeled garlic, minced
    1½ tablespoons brown rice vinegar
    1½ tablespoons flax oil
    2 teaspoons agave nectar
    1 tablespoon sesame seeds

Slice the cucumbers about ⅛ inch thick, discarding the ends. Put in a colander in the sink and sprinkle with 1 teaspoon of the salt. Toss well. Let drain for about 20 minutes. Rinse well. Pat dry with a towel.

Crush the chile flakes in a mortar. Add the garlic and remaining teaspoon of salt and crush together to form a mushy paste. Add the vinegar, oil, and agave nectar, stirring well. Scrape the mixture into a bowl. Add the cucumbers and sesame seeds. Mix thoroughly. Serve at once, in small bowls.

Per serving: calories: 92, protein: 1 g, fat: 6 g, carbohydrate: 8 g, fiber: 1 g, sodium: 536 mg, omega-3 fatty acids: 2.66 g

SPICY RED CABBAGE SLAW

Makes 4 servings

A little smoked paprika adds extra depth to an already potent dressing in this Mesoamerican incarnation of the ol' coleslaw. If you haven't made any Chipotle Mayonnaise (page 41), you can just use plain vegan mayonnaise and add a tablespoon or more of Chipotle Chile Purée (page 40). If you're thinking that the mortar and pestle bit looks a little strenuous, let me trot out my standard encouragement: Don't be intimidated! This takes about a minute and a half. It would actually be more difficult and take longer to use a blender because of the small quantity (not to mention the cleanup). Trust me, this is all very easy.

1 green bell pepper
3 cups shredded red cabbage (about ½ head)
1 red onion, quartered and thinly sliced
½ cup coarsely chopped fresh cilantro
1 carrot, grated
3 cloves peeled garlic
½ teaspoon sea salt
½ teaspoon pasilla or ancho chile powder
¼ teaspoon smoked paprika
1 tablespoon agave nectar
¼ cup Chipotle Mayonnaise (page 41)

Preheat the broiler.

Quarter the bell pepper and remove the seeds and membranes. Lay the pieces skin-side up on a baking sheet and place under the broiler for about 5 minutes, until the skin begins to blister and blacken. Immediately immerse in cold water. The skins should slip off easily, but if any parts are stubborn, scrape them off with a knife. Slice the pepper pieces about ¼ inch thick. Transfer them to a large bowl along with the cabbage, onion, cilantro, and carrot.

Pound the garlic in a mortar with the salt until it forms a mushy paste. Add the chile powder and paprika and work it into the paste. Add the agave nectar and incorporate. Scrape the pestle with a rubber spatula and gather the mixture in the mortar. Add the Chipotle Mayonnaise and fold it in. Scrape the mixture into the bowl with the vegetables and mix until well combined. Serve at once, in small bowls, or refrigerate until ready to eat.

Per serving: calories: 93, protein: 2 g, fat: 3 g, carbohydrate: 13 g, fiber: 3 g, sodium: 378 mg, omega-3 fatty acids: 0 g

GRILLED RADICCHIO SALAD

Makes 4 servings

This is irresistible. Strangely enough, grilling the radicchio tames its bitter side slightly. Combining it with a peppery green like arugula or watercress, roasted red pepper, and balsamic vinaigrette creates a vibrant, warm salad, with just enough complexity to dazzle the palate.

> 1 large bunch arugula or watercress
> 1 roasted red pepper
> ½ red onion, thinly sliced
> 2 heads radicchio
> 6 tablespoons extra-virgin olive oil
> 1 teaspoon sea salt
> ½ teaspoon freshly ground black pepper
> 2 tablespoons balsamic vinegar
> 1 tablespoon Roasted Garlic Purée (page 39), or 1 teaspoon minced garlic
> 1 teaspoon Dijon mustard
> ¼ cup chopped fresh parsley

Preheat a grill (outdoor or stovetop).

Remove and discard any coarse stems from the arugula or watercress and put the greens in a large bowl.

Quarter the red pepper, and then slice it about ½ inch thick. Put it in the bowl with the greens. Add the red onion.

Cut each head of radicchio in half lengthwise. Cut out the cores, leaving just enough to keep the radicchio in one piece. Brush with 2 tablespoons of the oil. Sprinkle with ½ teaspoon of the salt and ¼ teaspoon of the pepper. Put on the grill, cut-side down. Cook for about 2 minutes, turn over, and cook for 2 minutes longer. Transfer to a plate. Cover to keep warm.

To make the dressing, pour the remaining 4 tablespoons of oil into a small bowl. Add the vinegar, Roasted Garlic Purée, mustard, and the remaining ½ teaspoon of salt and ¼ teaspoon of pepper. Whisk until emulsified.

Cut the radicchio halves in half again lengthwise. Then slice them crosswise into ½-inch-wide strips. Add to the bowl with the greens and onion. Add the dressing and half of the parsley. Toss thoroughly.

Divide the salad among 4 plates, mounding it slightly. Garnish with a sprinkling of the remaining parsley. Serve at once, before the warmth of the radicchio wilts the greens.

Per serving: calories: 226, protein: 2 g, fat: 21 g, carbohydrate: 8 g, fiber: 2 g, sodium: 588 mg, omega-3 fatty acids: 0.15 g

SPICY DAIKON SALAD

Makes 4 servings

"Daikon" has such a powerful ring to it ("the courtiers all bowed low as the Daikon entered and took his seat on the dais"), and yet it is the mildest of all radishes. Never mind, I have given it some respectable potency by enrobing it in this chile-flecked sauce. Rock on, Daikon!

> 1 teaspoon crushed red chile flakes
> 1 clove peeled garlic, minced
> 1 teaspoon sea salt
> 1½ tablespoons brown rice vinegar
> 1½ tablespoons flax oil
> 2 teaspoons agave nectar
> 2 large carrots, shredded
> 1 small daikon, shredded
> 1 tablespoon black sesame seeds

Crush the chile flakes in a mortar. Add the garlic and salt and crush together to form a mushy paste. Add the vinegar, oil, and agave nectar, stirring well. Scrape the mixture into a bowl. Add the carrots, daikon, and sesame seeds. Mix thoroughly. Serve at once, in small bowls.

Per serving: calories: 107, protein: 1 g, fat: 6 g, carbohydrate: 9 g, fiber: 3 g, sodium: 583 mg, omega-3 fatty acids: 2.66 g

CAMPARI-BRAISED RADICCHIO SALAD WITH GRAPEFRUIT

Makes 4 servings   (See photo facing page 87.)

Campari, an Italian bitter aperitif made from herbs, enhances the bitterness of radicchio while paradoxically softening its edge. This salad must be assembled immediately before serving, as the heat from the braised radicchio will warm the grapefruit and cause the watercress to wilt fairly quickly. When properly done, however, the result is near transcendental.

> 2 heads radicchio
> 1 red onion
> 1/2 teaspoon freshly ground black pepper
> 1 bunch watercress
> 2 grapefruits
> 2 teaspoons agave nectar
> 2 teaspoons freshly squeezed lemon juice
> 1 teaspoon Dijon mustard
> 1 teaspoon sea salt
> 5 tablespoons extra-virgin olive oil
> 1/4 cup Campari

Quarter the radicchio lengthwise, but leave the core to help keep the leaves together. Cut each quarter crosswise into slices a little thinner than 1/2 inch thick. Discard the core pieces. Quarter and slice the onion the same way, but make the slices about 1/8 inch thick. Combine the radicchio and onion in a bowl. Season with the pepper and set aside.

Wash the watercress, and then crisp it in cold water for 5 to 10 minutes. Dry it in a salad spinner or roll it gently in a towel to absorb the excess water. Refrigerate until serving time.

Cut the tops and bottoms off the grapefruits. Put the grapefruits on a flat work surface and cut off the remaining peel by slicing downward, following the curve of the fruit. Cut between the membranes to loosen the segments. Transfer the segments to a bowl and set aside. Squeeze the remaining pieces to extract the juice, discarding any seeds. You should have about 1/2 cup of juice.

Pour 3 tablespoons of the grapefruit juice into a small bowl. Add the agave nectar, lemon juice, mustard, and ½ teaspoon of the salt. Whisk until well blended. Slowly add 3 tablespoons of the oil, whisking until emulsified.

Swirl the remaining 2 tablespoons of oil in a large skillet or wok over high heat. Add the radicchio and onion, stirring well until they begin to wilt. Add ¼ cup of the remaining grapefruit juice, the Campari, and the remaining ½ teaspoon of salt, stirring well. Continue to cook over high heat until the liquid is absorbed and the radicchio has thoroughly wilted, no more than 2 minutes. It should be tender-crisp. Remove from the heat.

Place the reserved watercress and grapefruit sections in a large bowl. Add the radicchio mixture and the dressing all at once, tossing gently but thoroughly. Divide among 4 plates, mounding it slightly. Serve at once.

Tip: If you're not familiar with Campari, it's about time. Bear in mind that bitter drinks are an acquired taste, and this one is definitely worth acquiring. Since this recipe only uses up a few tablespoons, you'll want to know how to properly dispose of the rest, so let me give you a few good ideas.

My favorite way is very simple: Pour a generous couple of ounces over 3 or 4 ice cubes in a tumbler. Cut one-quarter of an orange and squeeze the juice into the glass. Drop the squeezed peel into the glass and swirl the mixture gently. Sip.

Campari Soda: Fill a tall glass halfway with ice and pour in a shot or two of Campari. Fill with San Pellegrino (or another sparkling mineral water) or soda and stir.

Negroni Cocktail: Pour one shot each of Campari, sweet red vermouth, and gin over a few cubes of ice in a shaker. Add a twist of orange peel, shake, and strain. Alternatively, follow the same steps, but instead of using a shaker, simply pour over 3 or 4 ice cubes in a tumbler, swirl, and sip. Or chug and have another. Sorry—Campari brings out the enabler in me.

Per serving: calories: 245, protein: 3 g, fat: 17 g, carbohydrate: 19 g, fiber: 3 g, sodium: 588 mg, omega-3 fatty acids: 0.13 g

WARM WILD MUSHROOM SALAD

Makes 4 servings

Here is a light, satisfying appetizer. Remember to clean the mushrooms very thoroughly, since wild mushrooms often have a lot of grit embedded. Don't try this with reconstituted dried mushrooms! If you can't get fresh wild mushrooms, use a mixture of portobello, cremini, and button mushrooms and just call it Warm Mushroom Salad. When preparing the shallots, be careful to cut them cleanly with a very sharp knife, so all of the juices will stay inside and the pieces will be crisp.

1 pound mixed wild mushrooms (such as morels, chanterelles, porcinis, and/or shiitakes)
4 cups tender baby lettuce
¼ cup flax oil
2 tablespoons freshly squeezed lemon juice
1 teaspoon truffle-infused virgin olive oil
½ teaspoon sea salt
¼ teaspoon freshly ground black pepper
1 large pinch cayenne
2 tablespoons finely diced shallots
2 tablespoons snipped fresh chives

Wash the mushrooms well. Cut any large ones into bite-size pieces. Put them in a steamer. Steam over gently simmering water for about 5 minutes.

While the mushrooms are cooking, divide the lettuce among 4 plates, forming wide beds.

Put the flax oil, lemon juice, olive oil, salt, pepper, and cayenne in a large bowl. Whisk until well combined.

Remove the steamer insert and shake it gently to drain off any accumulated water on the mushrooms. Add the hot mushrooms to the oil mixture. Add the shallots and toss quickly. Spoon equally into the prepared beds of lettuce. Garnish with the chives. Serve at once.

Per serving: calories: 208, protein: 3 g, fat: 14 g, carbohydrate: 16 g, fiber: 3 g, sodium: 287 mg, omega-3 fatty acids: 7.11 g

PASTA AND
GRAINS

BROWN RICE SPAGHETTI WITH RADISH TOPS AND ARTICHOKES

Makes 4 servings

Pasta and artichokes are a heavenly pairing, no question, and brown rice spaghetti (a new love of mine) is by far the most effective of all the wheat-free pastas I've tried for creating a true *al dente* sensation. I first learned that radish tops were palatable from a Salvadoran coworker who used to take them off my hands and make omelets with them. I started using them myself and quickly understood their appeal. I've never thrown them away since.

> 1 pound brown rice spaghetti or other pasta
> ½ cup extra-virgin olive oil
> 1 tablespoon plus 1 teaspoon sea salt
> 7 cloves peeled garlic, sliced in half lengthwise, and then thinly sliced crosswise
> Green tops from 1 bunch radishes, coarsely chopped (about ½ cup, packed)
> 3½ cups artichoke hearts (packed in water), rinsed, drained, and cut in half lengthwise
> ¼ teaspoon freshly ground black pepper

Fill a large pot with water. Add 1 tablespoon of the oil and 1 tablespoon of the salt and bring to a boil. Add the spaghetti, stirring well to prevent sticking. Cook for 10 to 12 minutes, or until the spaghetti is *al dente*.

While the spaghetti is cooking, pour the remaining oil into a large sauté pan over medium-high heat. Add the garlic and cook, stirring constantly. As soon as the garlic begins to color, add the radish tops and stir until wilted. Add the artichoke hearts, the remaining teaspoon of salt, and the pepper. Stir until heated through.

Drain the spaghetti and quickly return it to the pot, retaining a bit of the cooking liquid. Add the hot artichoke mixture and toss well. Serve at once.

Per serving: calories: 652, protein: 18 g, fat: 24 g, carbohydrate: 88 g, fiber: 10 g, sodium: 782 mg, omega-3 fatty acids: 0.18 g

LOTUS ROOT SOBA NOODLES WITH TEKKA

Makes 2 to 4 servings

The earthy, smoky flavor of tekka lends an unusual power to the normally bland, retiring nature of soba noodles. In Japan, lotus root soba noodles (also called *renkon soba*) are usually served in a broth, but I prefer them in a light sauce. Probably that's the Italian in me, but mostly I think it's because I never really got the hang of the Japanese technique of tipping the bowl while using chopsticks to shove slippery noodles into my mouth and slurping them down along with the broth. It took me long enough to get to where I could eat *spaghetti al pomodoro* without looking like I'd participated in an ax murder. Guess I just figured I'd quit while I was ahead.

8 ounces lotus root soba noodles or other soba noodles
1 tablespoon sea salt
½ cup finely chopped shallots
3 tablespoons Garlic Oil (page 38)
2 tablespoons tekka
2 tablespoons mirin
1 tablespoon tamari
1 tablespoon chopped fresh parsley
1 teaspoon toasted sesame oil
1 teaspoon freshly squeezed lime juice
1 teaspoon Sriracha sauce (optional)

Fill a large pot with water. Add the salt and bring to a boil. Add the noodles, stirring to keep them from clumping.

While the noodles are cooking, combine the shallots with the Garlic Oil in a small bowl.

In a separate small bowl, combine the tekka, mirin, tamari, parsley, sesame oil, lime juice, and Sriracha sauce, if using.

Begin checking the noodles for doneness after about 4 minutes, as they should not take very long and they must not be allowed to overcook. They should be just past the chalky stage, but not too soft. As soon as they are done, drain them in a colander and return them to the pot. Add the shallot mixture and toss vigorously to mix well. Immediately add the tekka mixture and toss until evenly distributed. Serve at once.

Per serving: calories: 261, protein: 5 g, fat: 16 g, carbohydrate: 25 g, fiber: 2 g, sodium: 890 mg, omega-3 fatty acids: 3.6 g

ORECCHIETTE WITH HERB SAUCE

Makes 4 servings

The herb sauce is not traditional, so I suppose it will go with any number of different pasta shapes—in fact, there are few things it *won't* enhance—but *orecchiette*, which means "little ears" in Italian, are among the best for capturing sauces because of their somewhat intricate design. If you prefer, you can omit the pasta altogether and use the herb sauce to liven up a plate of steamed vegetables, potatoes, or even an open-face sandwich. Plan on using it fairly soon after making it, however, as it doesn't keep very well.

> 1 pound of orecchiette or your favorite pasta
> 4 tablespoons extra-virgin olive oil
> 1 tablespoon plus ½ teaspoon sea salt
> 1 cup packed baby spinach leaves
> 1 cup packed watercress leaves
> ¼ cup packed fresh tarragon leaves
> 2 tablespoons chopped shallot
> ¼ cup flax oil
> ½ teaspoon freshly ground black pepper

Fill a large pot with water. Add 1 tablespoon of the olive oil and 1 tablespoon of the salt and bring to a boil. Add the pasta, stirring well to prevent sticking. Cook for about 12 minutes, or until done to your liking. (This will vary according to the shape of the pasta as well as its composition.)

While the pasta is cooking, quickly proceed with making the sauce. Put the spinach, watercress, tarragon, and shallot in a blender. Process until smooth, adding a few teaspoons of water, if needed, to facilitate processing. With the motor running, add the flax oil through the cap opening in the lid. Then add the remaining ½ teaspoon of salt and the pepper.

As soon as the pasta is done, drain it in a colander (without shaking!) and quickly return it to the pot. Add the remaining 3 tablespoons of olive oil and shake the pot briskly to coat the pasta. Add the sauce and shake the pot again. Serve immediately! I believe it is a capital crime in Italy to let pasta get cold.

Per serving: calories: 387, protein: 6 g, fat: 25 g, carbohydrate: 33 g, fiber: 5 g, sodium: 282 mg, omega-3 fatty acids: 7.18 g

MUGWORT SOBA WITH GREEN CURRY

Makes 2 to 4 servings

Buckwheat noodles tend to be grainy and crumbly, but blended with mugwort yam, a traditional Japanese noodle combination, they hold up rather well. Tossing mugwort soba noodles (also called *yomogi soba*) with a little oil before adding the creamy sauce in this recipe helps keep them from sticking together, allowing for a pleasant contrast of textures. This will have plenty of bite for some people, but if you prefer a more fiery mouthful (as I do), I recommend an artful spattering of Sriracha sauce over the top to ramp it up.

8 ounces mugwort soba noodles or other soba noodles

1 tablespoon plus ½ teaspoon sea salt

1 cup coconut milk

1 bunch scallions, thinly sliced

½ cup chopped fresh cilantro

1 tablespoon Thai green curry paste

2 tablespoons almond, sesame, or flax oil

Fill a large pot with water. Add 1 tablespoon of the salt and bring to a boil. Add the noodles, stirring to keep them from clumping.

While the noodles are cooking, combine the coconut milk, scallions, cilantro, curry paste, and remaining ½ teaspoon of salt in a small bowl.

Begin checking the noodles for doneness after about 4 minutes, as they should not take very long and they must not be allowed to overcook. They should be just past the chalky stage, but not too soft. As soon as they are done, drain them in a colander and return them to the pot. Add the oil and toss vigorously to coat well. Immediately add the coconut milk mixture and toss well. Serve at once.

Per serving: calories: 327, protein: 6 g, fat: 26 g, carbohydrate: 15 g, fiber: 4 g, sodium: 419 mg, omega-3 fatty acids: 0 g

LINGUINE WITH SUNDRIED TOMATO SAUCE

Makes 4 servings

If you've invested the time to make a batch of Sundried Tomato Paste (page 43), this will take little more than the time required for a pot of water to boil. If you haven't, you can make it while the water comes to a boil and the result will be exactly the same. If you're in a desperate hurry, use spaghettini (also known as thin spaghetti), which, because it is half the thickness of the other options, will cook in half the time. Parsley adds a fresh taste, but if you don't have any, don't be concerned; the pasta will still be great without it.

> 1 pound linguine, spaghetti, or spaghettini
> ½ cup extra-virgin olive oil
> 1 tablespoon sea salt
> 1 cup Sundried Tomato Paste (page 43)
> 2 tablespoons chopped fresh parsley (optional)
> 1 tablespoon chopped fresh oregano, or 1 teaspoon dried
> 1 cup grated vegan parmesan cheese

Fill a large pot with water. Add 1 tablespoon of the oil and all of the salt and bring to a boil. Add the pasta, stirring constantly for about 1 minute to prevent sticking. Cook for about 9 minutes, or until the pasta is *al dente*. Pour into a colander to drain, but do not shake the colander. Immediately return the pasta to the pot and add the remaining olive oil. Shake the pot to coat the pasta. Add the Sundried Tomato Paste, parsley, if using, and oregano. Stir well to distribute thoroughly.

Divide among 4 plates. Serve at once, with the vegan parmesan cheese on the side.

Per serving: calories: 668, protein: 21 g, fat: 47 g, carbohydrate: 51 g, fiber: 4 g, sodium: 1,051 mg, omega-3 fatty acids: 0.24 g

SOBA NOODLES WITH MUSHROOMS

Makes 4 servings

Buckwheat soba noodles are delicious with mushrooms, including shiitake and oyster. Maitake mushrooms are pretty rare, but if you happen to find any, by all means add them to the mix. Fresh soba noodles can be bought in vacuum-sealed packages at many natural food stores and Asian markets. If you are unable to locate any, you can use dried soba noodles, but you will need to boil them first. Be sure to remove them from the boiling water before they are thoroughly cooked, as they will continue to cook in the sauce.

3 tablespoons tamari
1 tablespoon mirin
1 tablespoon dry sherry
1 tablespoon freshly squeezed lime juice
1 tablespoon dark agave nectar
2 teaspoons cornstarch
1 teaspoon Sriracha sauce
1 tablespoon toasted sesame oil
12 ounces fresh soba noodles
4 ounces shiitake mushrooms, sliced
4 ounces oyster mushrooms, sliced
½ cup dulse, soaked in room-temperature water for 2 minutes, drained, and coarsely chopped
1 bunch scallions, sliced on a diagonal
1 tablespoon sesame seeds

Bring a large pot of water to a boil.

Combine the tamari, mirin, sherry, lime juice, agave nectar, cornstarch, and Sriracha sauce in a small bowl.

Heat the oil in a large wok and swirl to coat. Grasp the soba noodles with a pair of tongs and dip them into the boiling water to loosen them. Immediately lift the noodles out of the water and put them into the hot wok. Stir well. Add the shiitake and oyster mushrooms and cook and stir for about 1 minute.

Swirl the tamari mixture and add it to the wok. Cook and stir until the mushrooms wilt slightly and the sauce thickens. Add the dulse, scallions, and sesame seeds, stirring and tossing until evenly distributed. Serve at once.

Per serving: calories: 202, protein: 6g, fat: 5 g, carbohydrate: 32 g, fiber: 3 g, sodium: 768 mg, omega-3 fatty acids: 0 g

STROZZAPRETI WITH MUSHROOMS

Makes 4 servings   (See photo between pages 134 and 135.)

You gotta love Italians—the name of this oddly twisted shape of pasta, *strozza-preti*, means "priest stranglers." One wonders what sort of passive-aggressive activity is implicit there. For this dish, I chose whole-grain strozzapreti made from farro, a delicious relative of wheat grown in Northern Italy. The grain itself is wonderful and worth trying sometime; but, sadly, it takes too long to cook for a recipe in this book. Any mushrooms you can find fresh will be good for this, although wild mushrooms have spectacularly rich flavors.

> ½ pound of strozzapreti di farro or your favorite pasta
> ¼ cup plus 1 tablespoon extra-virgin olive oil
> 1 tablespoon plus ½ teaspoon sea salt
> ½ cup chopped shallots
> 2 pounds mixed mushrooms (see tip)
> 1 vegetable bouillon cube
> 1 tablespoon porcini mushroom powder (optional)
> ½ teaspoon freshly ground black pepper
> ½ cup dry Marsala, dry sherry, or tawny port
> ¼ cup flax oil
> 2 tablespoons freshly squeezed lemon juice
> 2 tablespoons chopped fresh parsley
> Vegan parmesan cheese (optional)

Fill a large pot with water. Add 1 tablespoon of the oil and 1 tablespoon of the salt and bring to a boil. Add the pasta, stirring well to prevent sticking. Cook for about 12 minutes, or until done to your liking. (This will vary according to the shape of the pasta as well as its composition.)

While the pasta is cooking, quickly proceed with making the sauce. Heat the remaining ¼ cup of olive oil in a large pot. Add the shallots and cook and stir for about 2 minutes, until softened and lightly colored. Add the mushrooms and stir well. Cover the pot until the mushrooms release their liquid, about 1 minute. Remove the cover and add the bouillon cube, mushroom powder, if using, remaining ½ teaspoon of salt, and pepper. Stir well. Cook for 5 minutes, or until the liquid is absorbed and the mushrooms begin to brown a bit. Add the Marsala, stirring to incorporate any browned bits into the sauce.

As soon as the pasta is done, drain it in a colander (without shaking!). Quickly add the pasta to the pot of mushrooms. Shake the pot back and forth to toss the pasta into the sauce. Remove from the heat and add the flax oil, lemon juice, and parsley, shaking the pot back and forth to mix well. Serve at once, accompanied (if you wish) by your favorite vegan parmesan cheese.

Tip: Good mushroom choices for this recipe include button, chanterelle, cremini, morel, porcini, and/or shiitake.

Per serving: calories: 487, protein: 8 g, fat: 30 g, carbohydrate: 48 g, fiber: 7 g, sodium: 303 mg, omega-3 fatty acids: 7.21g

FASTA PASTA E FAGIOLI

Makes 4 to 6 servings (enough for 2 to 3 Italians)

Pasta e fagioli (pasta and beans) is quintessential comfort food, satisfying to the young and old. It usually takes a *mamma* hours to make, as the beans cannot be rushed. The traditional beans used for this are Italian borlotti, which are about the biggest beans around. If you have a good Italian deli near you, see if they carry canned borlotti beans. If not, the next best are cannellini. A third option, believe it or not, would be pinto beans, which aren't too wildly different from borlotti. (Just don't repeat this in front of any Italians!) Serve this in shallow soup bowls, accompanied by your favorite vegan parmesan cheese and some crusty Italian bread.

8 ounces tubetti (look for brown rice or farro tubetti, if you can find it)
5 tablespoons extra-virgin olive oil
1 tablespoon plus ½ teaspoon sea salt
1 small yellow or white onion, coarsely chopped
2 stalks celery, coarsely chopped
7 cloves peeled garlic
1 cup crushed tomatoes or tomato purée
½ teaspoon freshly ground black pepper
1 can (25 ounces) cannellini or pinto beans
⅓ cup fresh basil leaves, torn into fairly small pieces

Fill a large pot with water. Add 1 tablespoon of the oil and 1 tablespoon of the salt and bring to a boil. Add the tubetti, stirring well to prevent sticking. Cook for about 7 minutes. (The tubetti should still be somewhat firm, as they will finish cooking in the sauce.)

While the water is coming to a boil and the tubetti are cooking, make the sauce. Put the onion, celery, and garlic in a food processor. Pulse until very finely chopped (it should be almost a purée). Heat the remaining 4 table-spoons of olive oil in a large pot. Add the onion mixture, stirring constantly for about 4 minutes. (The aroma will be intoxicating.) Add the tomatoes, the remaining ½ teaspoon of salt, and the pepper. Cook over medium heat for about 10 minutes. Add the beans and bring to a simmer over medium heat. By now the tubetti should be done.

Drain the tubetti in a colander (without shaking!). Quickly add the tubetti to the beans and tomatoes along with the basil. The mixture should be fairly loose at this point, but as the pasta finishes cooking, in 1 or 2 minutes, it will thicken to a perfect consistency—a slightly soupy sauce with pasta and beans still slipping around independent of one another. Serve at once.

Tip: If the sauce gets too thick and the dish seizes up, add just a little hot water and shake the pot to loosen it up again. Don't do this too many times, however, or the pasta will soak up too much liquid and become mushy.

Per serving: calories: 396, protein: 12 g, fat: 13 g, carbohydrate: 54 g, fiber: 5 g, sodium: 420 mg, omega-3 fatty acids: 0.09g

TOFU AND SOBA NOODLES WITH HOT-SWEET-SOUR-PUNGENT SAUCE

Makes 4 servings   (See photo facing page 134.)

Don't worry if you're not a fan of spicy food; this sauce will not suffer significantly if you omit or greatly reduce the amount of Sriracha sauce (at least not as much as you might suffer if you left it in). Just call it Sweet-Sour-Pungent Sauce and act normal.

- ¾ cup tomato purée
- ½ cup hoisin sauce
- ¼ cup tamari
- ¼ cup brown rice vinegar
- ¼ cup dark agave nectar
- 12 cloves peeled garlic
- 1 tablespoon Sriracha sauce
- ½ teaspoon sea salt
- ¼ cup flax oil
- 8 ounces buckwheat soba noodles
- 1 pound extra-firm fresh tofu, cut into ½-inch cubes
- 1 bunch scallions, thinly sliced on a diagonal

Bring a large pot of water to a boil.

Put the tomato purée, hoisin sauce, tamari, vinegar, agave nectar, garlic, Sriracha sauce, and salt in a blender. Process until smooth. Pour into a large saucepan. Simmer over medium heat until the sauce is just thick enough to coat the spoon. Add the tofu pieces and warm through, stirring gently occasionally.

While the sauce is cooking, add the noodles to the pot of boiling water, stirring well to prevent sticking. Cook until just barely done, about 8 minutes. Drain in a colander and return to the pot. Add the flax oil, shaking the pot to coat the noodles. Add the sauce and tofu, shaking the pot and stirring gently to coat the noodles.

Divide among 4 plates. Top with the scallions. Serve at once.

Per serving: calories: 600, protein: 27 g, fat: 20 g, carbohydrate: 77 g, fiber: 6 g, sodium: 2,105 mg, omega-3 fatty acids: 7.1 g

BROWN RICE AND CARROTS WITH NATTO MISO

Makes 4 servings

When I make brown rice, I always make more than enough so I can use it the next day. That saves time and gives me a platform to work other flavors and textures into this sublime staple. The natural sweetness of brown rice is enhanced here by carrots braised with sake, tamari, and a touch of maple syrup. Serving it with natto miso (a traditional macrobiotic condiment made with barley, barley malt, ginger, and sea vegetables) may be gratuitous (my middle name), but so be it. Adding a dab of tahini combines with the rice to make a complete protein, and the combination is lip-smacking delicious.

> 6 to 8 thin carrots
> 2 teaspoons sesame oil
> 2 teaspoons maple syrup
> 1 tablespoon tamari, plus additional for serving
> ¼ cup sake or dry sherry
> 4 cups cooked brown rice (see page 46)
> Natto miso
> Tahini

Cut the carrots on a diagonal, rolling them with a one-quarter turn after each cut to create interesting uneven shapes. (They will vaguely resemble the trimmings from a hand-sharpened pencil.)

Heat the oil in a large sauté pan and add the carrots. Shake the pan and stir constantly to lightly sear the carrots. When the edges begin to color a bit, add the maple syrup. Continue cooking for 1 or 2 minutes, until all the liquid has cooked off and the carrots have acquired a sticky glaze. Add the tablespoon of tamari and repeat this procedure, shaking the pan and stirring until the carrots are almost dry. Add the sake, shake the pan, and cover tightly. Turn the heat down to low and cook for 7 to 10 minutes, or until the sake is nearly absorbed and the carrots are tender-crisp. Turn the heat up to high and add the rice, stirring until well mixed and heated through. Serve at once, with a dispenser of tamari and bowls of natto miso and tahini on the side.

Per serving: calories: 392, protein: 10 g, fat: 6 g, carbohydrate: 65 g, fiber: 8 g, sodium: 337 mg, omega-3 fatty acids: 0 g

SPAGHETTI WITH OLIVES AND LEMON

Makes 4 servings

Spaghetti with lemon and linguine with olives are two of my favorite Italian classics. I've taken a bit of a risk here by using brown rice pasta (*porca miseria!*) and combining them into one—not a culinary risk, mind you, but a mortal risk, for Italians take food very seriously. I think a jury of my peers would suspend the sentence this one time, though. The sauce is positively unctuous, yet light, bright, and lemony. Yumma.

- 1 pound brown rice spaghetti or other pasta
- 1 tablespoon sea salt
- 1/3 cup plus 1 tablespoon extra-virgin olive oil
- 1 cup pitted kalamata olives
- 1/4 cup coarsely chopped fresh parsley
- 3 tablespoons Roasted Garlic Purée (page 39), or 4 cloves peeled garlic, chopped
- 3 tablespoons freshly squeezed lemon juice
- 2 teaspoons grated lemon zest
- 1/4 teaspoon freshly ground black pepper

Fill a large pot with water. Add the salt and 1 tablespoon of the olive oil and bring to a boil. Add the spaghetti, stirring to prevent sticking. Cook for 10 to 12 minutes, or until *al dente*.

While the spaghetti is cooking, put the olives, parsley, Roasted Garlic Purée, lemon juice, lemon zest, pepper, and the remaining 1/3 cup of olive oil in a food processor. Pulse until finely chopped, stopping to scrape down the sides of the work bowl as needed.

Drain the spaghetti in a colander (do not shake!). Quickly return the spaghetti to the pot. Add the olive mixture and toss well. Serve at once.

Per serving: calories: 616, protein: 16 g, fat: 23 g, carbohydrate: 84 g, fiber: 6 g, sodium: 312 mg, omega-3 fatty acids: 0.13 g

RED QUINOA WITH ZUCCHINI AND CORN

Makes 4 to 6 servings

Red quinoa is fairly new on the natural food scene. For those who are familiar with quinoa, this variety has a firmer, almost crunchy texture and a robust earthy flavor to match its rich rust color. Pairing it with zucchini, corn, and cilantro brings the exotic New World flavors to life. Even though my taste memory goes back much further than my first experience with quinoa, this combination is for me a pre-Columbian meld that makes perfect sense to my palate. However, if you can't find red quinoa, don't let that stop you. Just substitute with regular quinoa.

> 3 tablespoons extra-virgin olive oil
> 1 yellow onion, diced
> 2 zucchini, diced
> 7 cloves peeled garlic, minced
> 2 cups frozen corn
> 1 cup red quinoa, rinsed and drained
> 2 cups carrot juice
> 1 teaspoon sea salt
> 1 vegetable bouillon cube
> ½ cup chopped fresh cilantro

Heat the olive oil in a medium pot. Add the onion and cook and stir for about 1 minute, until it begins to soften. Add the zucchini and garlic and cook and stir for 2 minutes. Add the corn and quinoa and stir to mix thoroughly. Add the carrot juice, salt, and bouillon cube and bring to a boil. Decrease the heat, cover, and cook for 15 to 20 minutes, until the quinoa is tender. Stir in the cilantro. Serve at once.

Per serving: calories: 301, protein: 3 g, fat: 10 g, carbohydrate: 41 g, fiber: 6 g, sodium: 477 mg, omega-3 fatty acids: 0.06 g

GREEN QUINOA

Makes 4 to 6 servings

Originally this was a North African couscous dish, somewhat reminiscent of Middle Eastern tabouli but served warm. I've improvised a bit by substituting quinoa (a whole grain from the Andes) for the couscous, which is essentially a form of refined durum wheat pasta.

> 1 cup quinoa
> 2 cups water
> 1 vegetable bouillon cube
> ½ cup flax oil
> ½ cup extra-virgin olive oil
> ½ cup freshly squeezed lemon juice
> ½ teaspoon sea salt
> ½ teaspoon freshly ground black pepper
> 2 large bunches fresh mint leaves, finely chopped
> 2 bunches scallions, finely chopped
> 1 cucumber, seeded and finely chopped
> 8 ounces arugula, finely chopped

Put the quinoa in a fine sieve. Rinse it well under running water and drain. Transfer to a small pot. Add the water and bouillon cube and bring to a boil. Turn the heat down to medium-low, cover, and cook for 15 minutes, or until all the water has been absorbed. The quinoa grains should be fully opened, giving the appearance of having "sprouted."

Whisk the flax oil, olive oil, lemon juice, salt, and pepper in a large bowl. Add the quinoa, mint, scallions, cucumber, and arugula. Toss until thoroughly mixed. Serve at once, while still warm.

Per serving: calories: 547, protein: 7 g, fat: 45 g, carbohydrate: 26 g, fiber: 5 g, sodium: 245 mg, omega-3 fatty acids: 12 g

RED PALM RICE

Makes 4 servings

As quick and easy as this is to make, the unique aroma and rich, complex flavor make it a potent accompaniment for even the most assertive of spicy dishes. Try it with Spicy Black Beans (page 152). If you have trouble finding red palm oil, you can still get a tasty dish by substituting with coconut oil.

1 cup basmati rice
2 tablespoons extra-virgin red palm oil or coconut oil
2 shallots, coarsely chopped
1 vegetable bouillon cube
1 cup carrot juice
1 cup water
½ teaspoon sea salt
1 bunch scallions, thinly sliced on a diagonal

Wash the rice gently in several changes of water, until no cloudiness remains. Drain thoroughly.

Heat the oil in a small pot. Add the shallots and cook, stirring briskly to prevent browning, until they have softened, about 2 minutes. Add the rice and stir gently to coat, taking care to prevent the grains from breaking. Crumble the vegetable bouillon cube over the rice, and then stir in the carrot juice, water, and salt. Bring to a boil, turn the heat down to the lowest setting, cover, and cook for 12 minutes. The rice should be perfectly cooked at this point, but if any liquid remains, cook for 2 minutes longer. Uncover, add the scallions, and fluff the grains gently with a rice paddle or silicone spatula. Serve at once.

Per serving: calories: 227, protein: 4 g, fat: 7 g, carbohydrate: 36 g, fiber: 3 g, sodium: 305 mg, omega-3 fatty acids: 0 g

HOMINY HASH

Makes 4 servings

I'll be honest with you, this dish looked like a catastrophic disaster halfway through the first run. I really thought it was going to be a failed experiment. As I've said many times, I don't favor imitations, especially ones that mimic something I've decided not to eat. But I have to admit, this dish turned out quite well. I ate my whole serving, down to the last bit. 'Nuff said.

    4 tablespoons extra-virgin olive oil
    4 (3-ounce) vegan Italian sausages, casings removed
    1 red onion, finely diced
    2 stalks celery, finely diced
    1 green bell pepper, finely diced
    1 can (15 ounces) white hominy, drained
    ½ cup tomato purée
    ½ teaspoon sea salt
    ¼ teaspoon freshly ground black pepper
    2 tablespoons chopped fresh parsley
    ½ cup Garlic Oil (page 38)
    Sriracha sauce (optional)

Put 2 tablespoons of the olive oil in a large sauté pan over high heat. Crumble the sausage into the pan and cook, stirring constantly, until it has browned lightly, about 2 minutes. Do not overcook. Transfer to a plate. Cover to keep warm.

Return the pan to the heat and add the remaining 2 tablespoons of olive oil. Add the onion and cook, stirring constantly, for 1 to 2 minutes, until softened. Add the celery and bell pepper and cook and stir for 2 minutes. Add the hominy and cook and stir for 2 minutes. Add the tomato purée, salt, and pepper, stirring to combine. Cover the pan, decrease the heat to medium, and cook for 5 minutes, or until the vegetables are tender.

Add the reserved sausage and the parsley, stirring well until the mixture has warmed through. Serve at once, with the Garlic Oil and Sriracha sauce on the side.

Per serving: calories: 540, protein: 8 g, fat: 46 g, carbohydrate: 21 g, fiber: 6 g, sodium: 782 mg, omega-3 fatty acids: 7.3 g

VEGETABLES AND LEGUMES

ASPARAGUS WITH CANNELLINI

Makes 4 servings   (See photo between pages 134 and 135.)

This is one of those Mediterranean-style dishes that are perfect served hot, at room temperature, or cold—wonderfully versatile for entertaining. Throwing the tomato and basil in at the end, off the heat, is the secret to the success of this feat of flavor and texture. If at all possible, use freshly picked, vine-ripened tomatoes and very fresh, verdant basil; even the most pedestrian can of cannellini beans will magically come to life under the touch of these two ingredients alone.

1 tablespoon plus ¼ teaspoons sea salt
2 tablespoons extra-virgin olive oil
1 cup finely diced red onion
2 cloves peeled garlic
1 can (15 ounces) cannellini beans, with liquid
½ teaspoon red wine vinegar
¼ teaspoon freshly ground black pepper
1 pound asparagus spears, trimmed uniformly to about 6 inches in length
1 medium-size ripe tomato, cut into ½-inch dice
¼ cup coarsely chopped fresh basil
2 tablespoons flax oil
1 tablespoon snipped fresh chives (optional)

Fill a large pot with water. Add 1 tablespoon of the salt. Cover and bring to a boil over high heat.

Meanwhile, put the olive oil in a large pan over medium-low heat. Add the onion, stirring well. After 1 to 2 minutes, when the onion juices begin to flow, squeeze the garlic through a garlic press directly into the pan. Add the cannellini beans and their liquid along with the vinegar, pepper, and remaining ¼ teaspoon of salt. Stir thoroughly but gently, to avoid crushing any of the beans. Bring to a simmer, and then decrease the heat to very low and cover. Continue to cook, stirring often, while you prepare the asparagus.

When the pot of water comes to a rolling boil, drop in the whole asparagus spears and stir once. Depending on the thickness of the asparagus, they should be just tender-crisp in about 1 minute. When they are done to your satisfaction, drain well.

Remove the beans from the heat and stir in the tomato, basil, and flax oil.

Divide the asparagus among 4 plates. Top with the bean mixture. Garnish with the chives, if using. Serve at once.

Per serving: calories: 293, protein: 12 g, fat: 14 g, carbohydrate: 24 g, fiber: 9 g, sodium: 155 mg, omega-3 fatty acids: 3.6 g

ASPARAGUS WITH SESAME SEEDS

Makes 4 servings

This is a variant of a classic Chinese dish. The goal is to cook it as quickly as possible, so the asparagus stay crisp. This goes well with brown rice, but it also makes a succulent appetizer. If you like spicy food, try throwing a teaspoon or two of crushed red chile flakes into the pan, right after the asparagus.

1½ pounds asparagus
2 tablespoons tamari
1 tablespoon mirin
1 teaspoon toasted sesame oil
1 teaspoon hoisin sauce
1 teaspoon cornstarch
1 tablespoon sesame oil
2 tablespoons sesame seeds

Wash the asparagus well, breaking off and discarding the tough, woody ends. Cut the asparagus into 2-inch lengths. Put the pieces in a bowl of cold water and set aside. This will refresh and crisp the asparagus.

Combine the tamari, mirin, toasted sesame oil, hoisin sauce, and cornstarch in a small bowl.

Heat a large wok over high heat. Drain the asparagus thoroughly. Add the sesame oil to the wok and swirl to coat. Immediately add the asparagus and stir briskly. The asparagus will hiss furiously and turn bright green. Continue stirring and add the tamari mixture. The sauce will thicken in about 1 minute. As soon as it begins to coat the asparagus, add the sesame seeds and stir well. Serve at once.

Per serving: calories: 116, protein: 6 g, fat: 6 g, carbohydrate: 8 g, fiber: 4 g, sodium: 545 mg, omega-3 fatty acids: 0 g

ROASTED EGGPLANT WITH SWEET MISO

Makes 4 servings

Eggplant and miso are a traditional Japanese combination. The pomegranate molasses is heresy. Sosumi.

  1 small to medium-size eggplant
  3 tablespoons extra-virgin olive oil
  3 tablespoons mellow white miso
  1 tablespoon pomegranate molasses
  1 tablespoon sake or dry sherry
  1 teaspoon freshly grated orange zest
  ¼ cup finely diced shallots

Preheat the oven to 450 degrees F. Line a baking sheet with parchment paper.

Cut the eggplant into slices about ½ inch thick. Brush the slices on both sides with 2 tablespoons of the oil and arrange them on the prepared baking sheet. Bake for about 10 minutes.

While the eggplant slices are baking, combine the remaining tablespoon of oil, miso, pomegranate molasses, sake, and orange zest in a small bowl and mix well. Add the shallots and stir thoroughly.

Remove the eggplant slices from the oven and spread the tops with the miso mixture. Return to the oven and bake for 15 minutes longer, or until tender. Serve at once.

Per serving: calories: 154, protein: 2 g, fat: 11 g, carbohydrate: 9 g, fiber: 3 g, sodium: 313 mg, omega-3 fatty acids: 0.08 g

BLAZING PINTO BEANS

Makes 4 servings

Pinto beans are comparatively large and creamy as beans go, making them ideal candidates for a blast of heat. Normally, I would dress them in freshly chopped cilantro with a splash of lime juice, but I found that smoked paprika, lemon juice, and sliced scallions do them just as much good. If these are too blazing for you, just cut back on the Chipotle Chile Purée.

2 tablespoons extra-virgin olive oil
½ red onion, finely diced
1 green bell pepper, finely diced
1 stalk celery, finely diced
4 cloves peeled garlic, minced
3 tablespoons Chipotle Chile Purée (page 40)
½ teaspoon sea salt
½ teaspoon smoked paprika
1 can (25 ounces) pinto beans, with liquid
1 bunch scallions, thinly sliced
2 tablespoons freshly squeezed lemon juice

Put the oil in a large pot over high heat. Add the onion and cook and stir for 1 to 2 minutes, until softened. Add the bell pepper, celery, and garlic and cook and stir for 2 minutes. Add the Chipotle Chile Purée, salt, paprika, and the liquid from the beans. Bring to a simmer, turn the heat down to low, and cover the pot. Cook for about 10 minutes, until the vegetables are tender, checking once or twice to make sure there is enough liquid to prevent sticking. If the mixture becomes too dry or thick, add a little water.

When the vegetables are done, add the beans, increase the heat to medium-high, and warm through. Remove from the heat and stir in the scallions and lemon juice. Serve at once.

Per serving: calories: 234, protein: 9 g, fat: 8 g, carbohydrate: 23 g, fiber: 10 g, sodium: 907 mg, omega-3 fatty acids: 0.05 g

Facing this page: Tofu and Soba Noodles with Hot-Sweet-Sour-Pungent Sauce, 122;

Miso-Red Curry Slaw, 98–99

Following page: Strozzapreti with Mushrooms, 118–119

BALSAMIC MUSHROOMS

Makes 4 servings

If you like mushrooms, you'll love these. Their earthy flavor is highlighted by just a little acidity from the balsamic vinegar, tamed by a touch of dark amber agave nectar. A fast and easy treat— washing the mushrooms is the hardest part!

- 1 pound mushrooms, preferably cremini or baby portobello
- 3 tablespoons extra-virgin olive oil
- ½ cup finely diced shallots
- 2 tablespoons balsamic vinegar
- 1 tablespoon dark agave nectar
- 1 teaspoon chopped fresh thyme, or ¼ teaspoon dried
- ¾ teaspoon sea salt
- ½ teaspoon freshly ground black pepper

Wash the mushrooms well and pat them dry. Quarter them, taking care to keep the stems attached.

Heat the oil in a large pan over high heat. Add the shallots and cook for about 2 minutes, stirring constantly. Add the mushrooms and stir well. Cover the pan and cook until the mushrooms begin to release their liquid, about 1 minute. Remove the cover and cook until the liquid is absorbed, about 5 minutes. Add the vinegar, agave nectar, thyme, salt, and pepper. Cook and stir for 1 to 2 minutes, until the mushrooms are lightly glazed with a smooth sauce. Serve at once.

Per serving: calories: 186, protein: 2 g, fat: 10 g, carbohydrate: 21 g, fiber: 3 g, sodium: 9 mg, omega-3 fatty acids: 0.08 g

Facing this page: Chocolate Pots de Crème, 159; Mangoes and Lychees with Mint, 160–161

Previous page: Asparagus with Cannellini , 130–131

BROCCOLI STEM AND GARBANZO CURRY

Makes 4 servings

I don't know about you, but I never want to eat the fat stems of the broccoli at the same time as the tops. They just seem like two different vegetables. On the other hand, it's a shame to throw the stems out, because they're just as good in their own way. This is one way to resolve that dilemma. Please don't rat me out to my Indian friends—this is anything but authentic. I'm trying to keep the recipe to under thirty minutes, so there you have it.

> 6 broccoli stems
> 10 cloves peeled garlic
> 2 tablespoons almond oil
> 1 red onion, finely diced
> 2 tablespoons curry powder
> 1 cup water
> 1 teaspoon sea salt
> 1 can (25 ounces) garbanzo beans, rinsed and drained
> 1 bunch fresh cilantro
> ½ cup thick coconut milk
> 1 (1-inch) piece fresh ginger, peeled and thinly sliced

Peel away the tough outer portion of the broccoli stems with a sharp paring knife. Quarter the stems lengthwise. Then cut them crosswise into ½-inch pieces, gathering them in a small bowl. Put the garlic through a garlic press and add it to the broccoli stems. Set aside.

Put the oil in a medium pot over high heat. Add the onion, stirring well. As soon as the onion is soft, about 2 minutes, stir in the broccoli stems, garlic, and curry powder. Cook and stir for 1 to 2 minutes. Add the water and salt, and bring to a boil. Decrease the heat slightly and simmer for 2 to 3 minutes, until the liquid is reduced to about 2 to 3 tablespoons and the vegetables are just tender. Stir in the garbanzo beans.

Keeping the cilantro in a bunch, wash it in cold water. Shake it well to re-move most of the water. Then wrap it in a paper towel and squeeze it dry. Lay the cilantro on a cutting board and chop across the bunch, beginning with the leaves. Discard the very ends of the stem tips. Divide the resulting pile roughly in half, separating the tender leaves from the tougher portion that includes the stems. Chop the leaves coarsely and set aside. Place the stem portion in a blender, add the coconut milk and ginger, and process until smooth. Pour into the pot with the broccoli and beans and stir well. The curry should be very green indeed. Reheat and reduce the liquid slightly, if necessary, to produce a pleasingly thick sauce. Stir in the reserved cilantro leaves and serve at once.

Per serving: calories: 435, protein: 20 g, fat: 18 g, carbohydrate: 43 g, fiber: 13 g, sodium: 598 mg, omega-3 fatty acids: 0 g

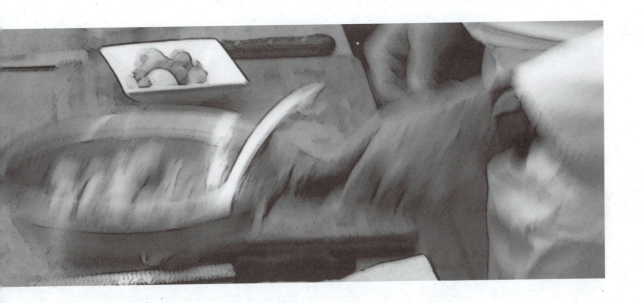

BITS 'N' PIECES GREEN CURRY

Makes 4 servings

Next time you look in your refrigerator and find a whole bunch of vegetables but not quite enough of any one, here's a good catch-all solution. The items included are just the ones I pulled out to create this recipe—you can use whatever you have. If anything seems essential to the success of this dish, then take note and make sure you always have it around. Serve this curry with plain basmati rice or Red Palm Rice (page 127).

        1 tablespoon coconut oil
        1 small broccoli top, broken into small florets
        3 broccoli stems, peeled and sliced on a diagonal
        2 small zucchini, sliced on a diagonal
        1 red bell pepper, cut into small strips
        ½ green bell pepper, cut into small strips
        ¼ head red cabbage, coarsely chopped
        2 tablespoons Thai green or red curry paste or Panang curry paste
        1 can (15 ounces) coconut milk
        1 bunch scallions, sliced on a diagonal
        1 cup coarsely chopped fresh basil or cilantro or a combination of both

Heat the coconut oil in a large pot or wok over high heat. Add the vegetables (in the order given, or the ones that take the longest to cook first, if you're using your own combination), a few at a time, stirring constantly to prevent any browning. Add the curry paste and cook for about 1 minute, stirring briskly. Add the coconut milk and bring to a boil. Remove from the heat and stir in the scallions and basil. Serve at once.

Per serving: calories: 293, protein: 5 g, fat: 27 g, carbohydrate: 10 g, fiber: 5 g, sodium: 181 mg, omega-3 fatty acids: 0 g

CELERY AND CORIANDER

Makes 4 servings

For a dish composed of four simple ingredients, this one is surprisingly complex and elegant. In the United States, we most often use the Spanish name for fresh coriander, cilantro, so I'll use it in the recipe for the sake of keeping everyone comfortable. For the best results, use only the large outer stalks of the celery and chop the cilantro very lightly.

8 stalks celery
2 tablespoons extra-virgin olive oil
Pinch sea salt
$\frac{1}{2}$ cup coarsely chopped fresh cilantro

Remove the outer layer of the celery stalks with a vegetable peeler. Slice the stalks on a diagonal, a little more than $\frac{1}{8}$ inch thick.

Heat the olive oil in a large sauté pan over medium-high heat. Add the celery and shake the pan to move it around in the oil. Adjust the heat so the celery sizzles lightly, but do not let it brown. Add the salt and continue to shake the pan frequently as the celery cooks. After about 15 minutes, check the celery for doneness. It should be tender but retain a little crunch. Once the celery is done, add the cilantro and stir well. Cook for 1 to 2 minutes longer, until the cilantro is just wilted and has released its aroma. Serve at once.

Per serving: calories: 73, protein: 1 g, fat: 7 g, carbohydrate: 1 g, fiber: 1 g, sodium: 65 mg, omega-3 fatty acids: 0.05 g

CHIPOTLE MUSHROOMS

Makes 4 servings

With an unusual combination of flavors for most people, this dish is an assertive accent even on a plate with beans. Cooking mushrooms with chipotle chiles and oregano is straightforward Mexican cuisine. The rest is mine.

1 pound button or cremini mushrooms, quartered
2 bunches scallions, sliced
¼ cup chopped shallots
2 tablespoons vegetable broth
Sea salt
Freshly ground black pepper
2 tablespoons Chipotle Chile Purée (page 40)
1 teaspoon dried oregano
2 tablespoons chopped fresh parsley
¼ cup flax oil
2 teaspoons freshly squeezed lime juice

Combine the mushrooms, scallions, shallots, and broth in a large sauté pan. Season with salt and pepper to taste. Cover with a tight-fitting lid and place over medium heat. As soon as you hear liquid bubbling, remove the cover, increase the heat to medium-high, and begin stirring. Add the Chipotle Chile Purée and oregano and continue stirring. As soon as all the liquid has been absorbed, about 3 minutes, stir in the parsley. Cook for 1 minute longer. Remove from the heat and add the oil and lime juice, shaking the pan to incorporate them into the mixture. Serve at once.

Per serving: calories: 200, protein: 3 g, fat: 13 g, carbohydrate: 17 g, fiber: 3 g, sodium: 81 mg, omega-3 fatty acids: 7.1 g

MASHED ALOO GOBI

Makes 4 servings

Aloo gobi (potatoes and cauliflower) is a classic Indian dish, and (full disclosure) this is far from it. However, this is a tasty alternative to the usual mashed potatoes. Of course, if you've got some properly prepared aloo gobi, you could mash it, and that would be both lightning fast and sublime (although it would also be a sad waste of perfectly good aloo gobi). This version is quick and yummy, so there you go.

1 tablespoon coconut oil
½ head cauliflower, coarsely chopped
1 tablespoon curry powder
1 teaspoon sea salt
1½ cups vegetable broth
3 russet potatoes
2 tablespoons chopped fresh cilantro (optional)

Put the oil in a large pot over high heat. When the oil is very hot, add the cauliflower. Cook and stir for a few minutes, until the cauliflower begins to brown lightly and emits an appealing aroma. Add the curry powder and salt, stirring well to combine thoroughly. Add the vegetable broth and bring to a boil. Decrease the heat, cover the pot, and simmer for 10 to 15 minutes, or until the cauliflower is tender.

Peel the potatoes, and then cut them into small pieces (about ¾ inch thick). Add them to the pot along with enough water to just cover them. Bring to a boil, decrease the heat, and cook, stirring occasionally, for about 15 minutes, or until the potatoes are very tender.

Drain the vegetables, reserving the broth in a small bowl, and return the vegetables to the pot. Mash thoroughly, adding some of the reserved broth as needed to create the desired consistency. Taste and add more salt, if needed. Stir in the cilantro, if using. Serve at once.

Per serving: calories: 160, protein: 4 g, fat: 4 g, carbohydrate: 25 g, fiber: 5 g, sodium: 582 mg, omega-3 fatty acids: 0 g

HERBED FINGERLING POTATOES

Makes about 4 servings

Fingerlings are interesting looking, but they're also very tasty, with a pleasant "new potato" skin and a texture reminiscent of Yukon gold potatoes. They come in a variety of colors, too, and are often sold as a mixture.

- 1½ pounds fingerling potatoes
- 3 tablespoons olive oil
- 2 tablespoons chopped fresh sage, rosemary, and thyme (in any combination)
- 4 cloves peeled garlic, finely chopped
- 1 teaspoon sea salt
- ½ teaspoon freshly ground black pepper

Bring a large pot of water to a boil.

Meanwhile, wash the potatoes, and cut any oversize ones into pieces that match the rest, for even cooking. When the water is boiling, add the potatoes and return to a boil. Decrease the heat slightly and cook for about 20 minutes, or until the potatoes are tender. Drain. Transfer to a bowl and keep covered.

Put the oil in the same pot over medium heat. Add the herbs, garlic, salt, and pepper. Cook and stir for about 1 minute, just until the garlic and herbs release their aroma. Add the warm potatoes and toss well to coat them with the herb mixture. Serve at once.

Per serving: calories: 236, protein: 3 g, fat: 10 g, carbohydrate: 34 g, fiber: 3 g, sodium: 542 mg, omega-3 fatty acids: 0.08 g

MASHED POTATOES WITH ROASTED GARLIC AND YELLOW PEPPERS

Makes 4 servings

Although the added flavor is fairly subtle, this is a delicious departure from the tired, old, pedestrian mashed potatoes to which we're all well accustomed. Not that there's anything wrong with mashed potatoes, but here they become a gourmet's treat as well as a gourmand's comfort food. Note that there is no fat in this dish (beyond the stowaway trace amount in the roasted garlic).

> 4 large russet potatoes
> 1 jar (15 ounces) roasted yellow peppers, rinsed and drained
> 2 tablespoons Roasted Garlic Purée (page 39)
> 1 teaspoon sea salt, plus more as needed
> 1/4 teaspoon freshly ground black pepper

Select a pot large enough to accommodate the potatoes amply, fill with water, and place in the sink. Peel the potatoes and drop them into the pot (they will displace the water). Pour some of the water out of the pot, leaving just enough to cover the potatoes. Remove the potatoes. Add 1 teaspoon of the salt to the water in the pot, cover, and bring to a boil over high heat. While the water is heating, cut the potatoes into small pieces and add them to the pot. Once all of the potatoes are in the pot, leave the cover off. Bring to a boil, and then lower the heat to maintain a simmer. Cook for about 20 minutes, or until very tender.

While the potatoes are cooking, place the peppers and Roasted Garlic Purée in a blender. Process until smooth.

When the potatoes are done, drain them thoroughly and return them to the pot. Begin mashing them with a potato masher. Then add the pepper mixture and mash until fairly smooth (a few small chunks will provide textural interest). Season with the pepper. Taste and add more salt, if needed. Reheat, stirring constantly to prevent sticking. Serve at once.

Per serving: calories: 161, protein: 4 g, fat: 0 g, carbohydrate: 37 g, fiber: 3 g, sodium: 541 mg, omega-3 fatty acids: 0 g

MISO AND GARLIC MASHED POTATOES

Makes 4 servings

Mashing a little miso into your potatoes adds a pleasant salty tang. Experiment with different kinds of miso, such as genmai (brown rice), mugi (barley), or any of the new combinations on the market. The first time I made this I used an unusual variety of miso made from garbanzo beans instead of the traditional soybeans. Be sure to add the flavorings after removing the potatoes from the heat so as not to kill the live enzymes in the miso or damage the omega-3 fats in the flax oil.

> 2 pounds russet potatoes
> ¼ cup mellow white miso
> ¼ cup flax oil
> 2 cloves peeled garlic, crushed in a garlic press
> ½ teaspoon sea salt
> ¼ teaspoon freshly ground black pepper
> 2 tablespoons snipped chives (optional)

Peel the potatoes and cut them into small chunks. Place them in a large pot and add water to cover by about 1 inch. Bring to a boil over high heat. Decrease the heat slightly, cover, and cook for 15 to 20 minutes, or until very tender. Slide the pot lid back just enough to allow the water to drain without spilling the potato chunks, and pour the water into a bowl.

Uncover the pot and mash the potatoes thoroughly. Keep the potatoes warm until you are ready to serve them (they are best served as soon as they are cooked). Just before serving, add the miso, oil, garlic, salt, and pepper and mash together thoroughly. Add just enough of the hot cooking water to achieve the desired consistency. Taste and adjust the seasonings, if needed. Stir in the chives, if using. Serve at once.

Per serving: calories: 352, protein: 6 g, fat: 14 g, carbohydrate: 50 g, fiber: 4 g, sodium: 686 mg, omega-3 fatty acids: 7.1 g

MOROCCAN VEGETABLE STEW

Makes 4 generous servings

The secret to this dish is ras el hanout, a uniquely Moroccan blend of spices that, once hard to find in America, is now widely available in specialty shops and many natural food stores. Bargains can also be found by shopping online. Traditionally, a stew like this would be served with couscous, but because that's actually a fancy form of refined wheat-flour pasta, you may prefer to serve it with a whole grain, such as quinoa. Pass a bowl of Hot Red Pepper Sauce (page 42) at the table.

- 2 tablespoons extra-virgin olive oil
- 1 large red onion, coarsely diced
- 1 large green bell pepper, coarsely diced
- 3 zucchini, cut into bite-size pieces
- 2 carrots, cut into bite-size pieces
- 7 cloves peeled garlic, sliced
- 1 tablespoon ras el hanout
- 1 teaspoon sea salt
- 1 can (28 ounces) peeled Italian tomatoes, cut in half lengthwise (reserve the juice)
- 1 can (15 ounces) garbanzo beans, rinsed and drained
- 1 vegetable bouillon cube
- 1 large pinch saffron threads

Put the olive oil in a large pot over high heat. Add the onion and cook and stir until it is lightly browned and beginning to soften, about 4 minutes. Add the bell pepper and cook and stir for about 2 minutes. Add the zucchini, carrots, garlic, ras el hanout, and salt, stirring well to coat the vegetables with the seasonings. Add the tomatoes and their juice, the garbanzo beans, bouillon cube, and saffron. Stir well. Decrease the heat, cover, and simmer for about 15 minutes, or until the vegetables are tender.

Per serving: calories: 256, protein: 10 g, fat: 9 g, carbohydrate: 28 g, fiber: 10 g, sodium: 859 mg, omega-3 fatty acids: 0.05 g

SEITAN WITH SNOW PEAS AND BEAN SPROUTS

Makes 4 servings

I've never been one for imitation meats (or imitation anything, for that matter), so I had never once tried seitan. But having committed myself to writing this book, I finally got around to using some in a dish or two. Look what I was missing! Turns out seitan isn't fake meat at all—it's just some wacky Japanese invention that happens to bear a vague similarity to meat (if you haven't had any for a while, maybe). To a Nippophile like me, this was a cool discovery. Don't let the number of ingredients scare you off. This is a very quick-and-easy dish to make. Once you've assembled everything, it'll all be over in a matter of about five minutes—and if you don't happen to have one or two of the items, just soldier on. The result will explode with flavor in your mouth anyway.

5 tablespoons tamari
1 tablespoon mirin
1 tablespoon dry sherry
1 teaspoon toasted sesame oil
1 teaspoon Sriracha sauce
$\frac{1}{4}$ teaspoon sea salt
2 teaspoons cornstarch or arrowroot
$\frac{1}{4}$ cup water
2 tablespoons sesame oil
8 ounces chicken-style seitan, drained well
8 ounces snow peas, strings removed
8 ounces mung bean sprouts
1 red bell pepper, cut into strips
2 tablespoons finely chopped fresh ginger
4 cloves peeled garlic, finely chopped
1 bunch scallions, sliced on a diagonal
$\frac{1}{2}$ bunch fresh cilantro, coarsely chopped

Combine the tamari, mirin, sherry, toasted sesame oil, Sriracha sauce, and salt in a small bowl. Stir together the cornstarch and water in a separate small bowl.

Swirl the sesame oil in a large pot or wok over high heat. Add the seitan and cook for 2 to 3 minutes, stirring occasionally, until lightly browned. Add the snow peas, bean sprouts, bell pepper, ginger, and garlic. Cook and stir for 1 minute. Add the tamari mixture and cook and stir for 1 minute. Add the cornstarch mixture and cook and stir until it thickens and forms a sauce, about 1 minute. Remove from the heat. Stir in the scallions and cilantro. Serve at once.

Per serving: calories: 356, protein: 48 g, fat: 9 g, carbohydrate: 18 g, fiber: 3 g, sodium: 1,367 mg, omega-3 fatty acids: 0 g

ODDS AND ENDS REDUX, À LA DEBORAH

Makes 4 servings

My sister is a gifted artist with some truly amazing talents; here's just one of them: Five minutes after someone looks in the fridge and complains there's nothing to eat, she'll have made at least three dishes that totally rock. Well, okay, maybe it'll take her twenty minutes, but you get the point. This isn't her recipe (she never writes down these one-shot deals), but it could have been. It's an example of something fast you can do with whatever remains in the larder. Trust me, you can always pull something awesome together if you have the eye, the taste, and the will. Of course, it helps if you've been eating well as a habit.

> 3 cooked ears of slightly dried out corn, rotten kernels dug out
> 1 slightly limp zucchini with a few moldy spots
> 1 red onion, the soft, slightly hairy half cut away
> 1/4 bunch slightly wilted cilantro, yellowed and mushy black parts removed
> 1 tablespoon extra-virgin olive oil
> 1 1/2 cups carrot juice, dangerously close to expiration date
> 4 cloves peeled garlic, minced or pressed
> 1/2 teaspoon sea salt
> 1/4 teaspoon freshly ground black pepper

Cut the corn kernels off the cobs directly into a small bowl.

Rub the moldy spots off the zucchini with the back of your thumbnail. Wash well. Cut into small dice about twice the size of the corn kernels.

Finely dice what's left of the onion.

Wash and dry the cilantro. Chop it coarsely.

Put the olive oil in a medium saucepan over high heat. Add the onion and cook and stir for 2 to 3 minutes, until it is soft and just beginning to color. Add the zucchini and cook and stir for 4 minutes. Add the reserved corn, carrot juice, garlic, salt, and pepper. Break up any clumps of corn with a wooden spoon. Bring to a boil, decrease the heat slightly, and cook until the carrot juice is absorbed and the vegetables are tender, about 7 minutes. Stir in the cilantro and you're done. See? There *was* something to eat in there.

Per serving: calories: 193, protein: 5 g, fat: 5 g, carbohydrate: 34 g, fiber: 4 g, sodium: 564 mg, omega-3 fatty acids: 0.03 g

PORTOBELLO MUSHROOMS WITH SCALLIONS AND PEAS

Makes 4 servings

I made the first version of this succulent dish with green garbanzos, which I loved (I grew up in Mexico, so I love all legumes), but my wife and son (gringos) didn't "get" my garbanzo obsession at all. They preferred the final version, with peas. This goes very nicely with brown rice cooked in a 50/50 combination of carrot juice and vegetable broth. Or, for a speedier meal, just add a few extra tablespoons of olive oil and toss it with pasta.

- 3 tablespoons extra-virgin olive oil
- 3 bunches scallions, cut into $1/4$-inch slices
- 4 cloves peeled garlic, finely chopped
- 3 portobello mushrooms, cut into $1/2$-inch dice
- $1 1/2$ cups frozen peas
- 1 tablespoon white wine
- 1 vegetable bouillon cube
- 1 teaspoon herbes de Provence
- $1/2$ teaspoon sea salt
- $1/4$ teaspoon freshly ground black pepper

Heat the olive oil in a large sauté pan over medium-high heat. Add the scallions and garlic and cook and stir for about 30 seconds. Add the mushrooms, peas, wine, bouillon cube, herbes de Provence, salt, and pepper. Stir well, cover, and cook for about 2 minutes. Remove the cover and cook, stirring often, for 2 minutes, or until the liquid has thickened to a light sauce. Serve at once.

Per serving: calories: 211, protein: 6 g, fat: 11 g, carbohydrate: 21 g, fiber: 7 g, sodium: 321 mg, omega-3 fatty acids: 0.08 g

SWEET-SOUR-HOT-PUNGENT LETTUCE AND TOFU

Makes 4 servings

The secret to this dish is to not overcook the lettuce. The combination of the fresh, crunchy iceberg lettuce, tender tofu, and intensely flavored sauce is unbelievable.

    1 head iceberg lettuce
    12 ounces extra-firm fresh tofu
    2 tablespoons agave nectar
    1 tablespoon tamarind paste concentrate
    1 tablespoon tamari
    2 teaspoons Sriracha sauce
    2 teaspoons cornstarch
    1 tablespoon water
    2 tablespoons almond oil
    6 cloves peeled garlic, thinly sliced
    1 bunch scallions, sliced
    1 tablespoon sesame seeds

Remove any wilted outer leaves from the lettuce. Rap the core end sharply on the kitchen counter. This should break the core loose so you can pull it out easily. Discard the core and cut the lettuce into 1½-inch cubes. Transfer to a large plate and set aside.

Cut the tofu into roughly ¾-inch cubes. Transfer to a large plate and set aside.

Combine the agave nectar, tamarind paste, tamari, and Sriracha sauce in a small bowl, stirring well. Stir the cornstarch and water together in a separate small bowl.

Put a large wok or pot over high heat and add the oil, swirling to coat the bottom. Add the garlic and cook and stir until lightly colored, about 1 minute. Add the lettuce and cook and stir for about 1 minute. Add the tamarind mixture and stir well. Add the cornstarch mixture and tofu, stirring gently to prevent the tofu from breaking. Cook and stir until the mixture thickens, about 1 minute.

Remove from the heat. Stir in half of the scallions and all of the sesame seeds. Divide among 4 plates. Garnish with the remaining scallions. Serve at once.

Per serving: calories: 222, protein: 12 g, fat: 13 g, carbohydrate: 15 g, fiber: 2 g, sodium: 380 mg, omega-3 fatty acids: 0 g

SPICY BLACK BEANS

Makes 4 servings

I grew up in Mexico, so when I make black beans I automatically want to give them a Mexican flavor. Since I have a hard time finding epazote (a unique herb used in cooking black beans, among other things) anywhere outside of Mexico, this is as close as I can get to the right stuff. Don't worry if you can't find pasilla chile powder—the Chipotle Chile Purée will provide plenty of authentic flavor. If you wish, pass a small dish of extra Chipotle Chile Purée at the table for people who might like their beans even hotter.

> 1 large white or red onion, finely diced
> 4 roma tomatoes, coarsely chopped
> 2 tablespoons Chipotle Chile Purée (page 40)
> 7 cloves peeled garlic
> 1 tablespoon pasilla chile powder (optional)
> ½ teaspoon sea salt
> 3 tablespoon extra-virgin olive oil
> 1 can (25 ounces) black beans, rinsed and drained
> 1 tablespoon freshly squeezed lime juice (optional)
> ¼ cup chopped fresh cilantro

Set aside half of the onion and put the other half in a blender. Add the tomatoes, Chipotle Chile Purée, garlic, chile powder, if using, and salt. Process until smooth.

Put the oil in a medium saucepan over high heat. Add the reserved onion and cook and stir for 2 to 3 minutes, until softened and just beginning to color. Add the blended tomato mixture and stir well. Cook on high heat for 5 to 7 minutes, until reduced to a fairly thick sauce. Add the beans and cook over medium heat for 4 to 5 minutes.

Remove from the heat and stir in the lime juice, if using. Serve at once, in bowls as a side dish or on a plate with rice and vegetables, garnished with a sprinkling of the cilantro.

Per serving: calories: 375, protein: 18 g, fat: 12 g, carbohydrate: 36 g, fiber: 18 g, sodium: 353 mg, omega-3 fatty acids: 0.08 g

ZUCCHINI AND RED BEANS

Makes 4 servings

There is something ancient about the combination of beans and squashes, an essence of cookery that speaks of a primeval drive to make the palate dance. That combination is vastly updated in this recipe, where elements that include spices and vegetables both pungent and succulent come together at a crossroad of Northwest African, Mesoamerican, and Asian influences. It's amazing to think that such a simple, earthy dish can actually cross time and distance and carry the story of so many peoples, complete with their songs, drums, and yearnings.

2 tablespoons extra-virgin olive oil
1 cup diced red onion
2 large zucchini, cut into ½-inch dice
1½ cups canned diced tomatoes, with juice
½ cup Roasted Garlic Purée (page 39)
1 teaspoon ras el hanout (preferably) or curry powder
½ teaspoon sea salt
1 can (15 ounces) red kidney beans (reserve the liquid)
½ cup coarsely chopped fresh cilantro

Heat the oil in a large pot over medium-high heat. Add the onion and cook and stir for about 1 minute. Add the zucchini and cook and stir for about 4 minutes.

While the vegetables are cooking, combine the tomatoes and Roasted Garlic Purée in a shallow bowl and mash together to form a slightly soupy mixture. The tomatoes should remain in pieces. Add to the onion and zucchini along with the ras el hanout and salt. Stir well. Decrease the heat to medium and cook for about 10 minutes. The zucchini should be just a bit tender. Increase the heat to high and add the beans along with about ¼ cup of their liquid. Cook for a few minutes longer, until the liquid is reduced and forms a light sauce.

Remove from the heat. Stir in the cilantro. Serve at once.

Per serving: calories: 262, protein: 11 g, fat: 8 g, carbohydrate: 33 g, fiber: 9 g, sodium: 897 mg, omega-3 fatty acids: 0.05 g

ZUCCHINI WITH TOMATOES

Makes 4 servings

One of the treasured taste memories from my childhood, *calabacita con jitomate* (zucchini with tomato), brings up an image of pure comfort food. Don't ask me why—most kids hate vegetables. Somehow the sweetness of this dish, with its mingled redolence of onion, garlic, and cinnamon, is just magical. I've messed with it a little to protect the omega-3s from the heat, but the essence remains. Try to find very small zucchini, because the larger they get, the tougher their skin gets, and the luscious zucchini flavor all but disappears. This is ambrosial served with plain basmati rice.

> 4 medium tomatoes, coarsely chopped
> 1 small to medium-size white onion, coarsely chopped
> 4 cloves peeled garlic
> ¼ teaspoon ground cinnamon
> 1½ pounds zucchini, quartered lengthwise and cut into ½-inch pieces
> ½ teaspoon sea salt
> ¼ teaspoon freshly ground black pepper
> ¼ cup flax oil

Combine the tomatoes, onion, garlic, and cinnamon in a blender. Process until smooth. Pour into a large skillet and bring to a simmer over medium-high heat. Add the zucchini, salt, and pepper and adjust the heat to maintain a simmer. Cook, stirring often, for 10 to 15 minutes, until the zucchini is tender and the tomato mixture has thickened to a sauce.

Remove from the heat. Add the oil and shake the pan to incorporate. *Sabor!*

Per serving: calories: 181, protein: 3 g, fat: 14 g, carbohydrate: 10 g, fiber: 4 g, sodium: 295 mg, omega-3 fatty acids: 7.1 g

BARBARA'S PINEAPPLE BABY BOK CHOY

Makes 4 servings

A very good friend of mine came up with this remarkably simple, fast, and delectable way to make baby bok choy. Her version called for clarified butter, but I found that coconut oil combines seamlessly with the flavors in this dish. It became an instant favorite. Make sure you select very fresh green bok choy.

>   4 baby bok choy
>   1 slice fresh pineapple, about ¾ inch thick
>   2 tablespoons coconut oil
>   1 to 2 tablespoons tamari

Lay the bok choy on a cutting board and cut across the leafy green part at roughly ¾-inch intervals, narrowing to about ¼-inch intervals as you reach the stem. This will help the bok choy cook evenly and allow for a more attractive presentation.

Cut the core out of the pineapple slice and discard it. Cut the pineapple flesh into roughly ⅜-inch dice.

Heat the coconut oil in a large sauté pan over high heat. Add the pineapple, stirring well. Cook and stir until the pineapple caramelizes and browns lightly, about 4 minutes. Add the bok choy and cook and stir for 1 to 2 minutes, until it is wilted. Add 1 tablespoon of the tamari and stir well. Taste and add more tamari, if needed. Serve at once.

Per serving: calories: 97, protein: 3 g, fat: 7 g, carbohydrate: 6 g, fiber: 2 g, sodium: 441 mg, omega-3 fatty acids: 0 g

BLACK BEANS, MUSHROOMS, AND BOK CHOY

Makes 4 servings

This turned out to be a combination I couldn't believe I hadn't thought of before. It was so richly real and obvious: where had I been all its life?

2 tablespoons coconut oil
¼ cup finely diced shallots
2 portobello mushrooms, cut into small cubes
2 tablespoons Thai red curry paste
¾ teaspoon sea salt
1 can (25 ounces) black beans, rinsed and drained
1 vegetable bouillon cube
1 tablespoon balsamic vinegar
1 tablespoon sake or dry sherry
2 heads baby bok choy, leaves coarsely chopped, stems thinly sliced
½ cup chopped fresh cilantro
1 tablespoon freshly squeezed lime juice

Heat the coconut oil in a large sauté pan over medium-high heat. Add the shallots and cook and stir for about 2 minutes. Add the mushrooms and cook and stir for 1 minute. Stir in the red curry paste and salt. Cover the pan and cook for 1 to 2 minutes, until the mushrooms have released their liquid. Remove the cover and add the beans, bouillon cube, vinegar, and sake, stirring well. Cook until most of the liquid has been absorbed, about 5 minutes. Add the bok choy and cook and stir for 2 minutes, or until the leaves have wilted and the stems are just tender. Remove from the heat and stir in the cilantro and lime juice. Serve at once. Wow, right?

Per serving: calories: 275, protein: 13 g, fat: 7 g, carbohydrate: 39 g, fiber: 11 g, sodium: 755 mg, omega-3 fatty acids: 0 g

SWEETS

AZTEC HOT CHOCOLATE

Makes 1 divine cup

If you've read Laura Esquivel's astonishing book *Like Water for Chocolate*, you may have wondered what the title was all about. Water is what chocolate has been dissolved in for millennia to make hot chocolate, that's all (except now you have to go back and reread the book to figure out the connection—sorry!). Before the Spaniards conquered Mexico, the Aztecs had never seen cattle (let alone milk), so their hot chocolate was naturally 100 percent vegan. Today, Mexican chocolate very often includes cinnamon, which is not native to the Americas, but agave nectar goes back to the time of the Toltecs, before the word "Aztec" even existed. I've tried a few different varieties of chile in my chocolate recipes, including ancho, chipotle, and pasilla, but I find a simple hot red chile like *chile de arbol* or cayenne gives it just enough heat without mud-dying the food of the gods. Be sure to use the best quality cocoa you can find!

    3 tablespoons Dutch-process cocoa powder
    2 tablespoons agave nectar
    ¼ teaspoon ground cinnamon
    ¼ teaspoon Indian hot red chile powder or cayenne
    1 cup boiling water

Put the cocoa, agave nectar, cinnamon, and chile powder in a coffee mug. Pour in the boiling water and stir vigorously. Drink. Feel awe and gratitude.

Per one-cup serving: calories: 157, protein: 3 g, fat: 2 g, carbohydrate: 36 g, fiber: 5 g, sodium: 3 mg, omega-3 fatty acids: 0 g

CHOCOLATE POTS DE CRÈME

Makes 4 servings   (See photo facing page 135.)

Where there's a will, there's a way. I never would have imagined that I could get the creamy texture of a classic pot de crème without the cream and egg yolks, but here (*voilà!*) it is. You're welcome. The basil and pepper add an ethereal flavor to this dish that most people won't be able to put their finger on but will still know is there. I like the idea of delighting their palates and messing with their heads with the same gesture. It's fun.

    1 can (14 ounces) coconut milk
    5 ounces bittersweet chocolate, coarsely chopped
    ½ cup fresh basil leaves, coarsely torn
    2 tablespoons agave nectar
    1 teaspoon finely grated orange zest
    ½ teaspoon vanilla extract, preferably Tahitian
    ¼ teaspoon crushed Javanese comet's tail peppercorns or
        black peppercorns

Put the coconut milk in a small pot over medium-high heat and bring to a simmer.

Put the chocolate in a blender and pour the hot coconut milk over it. Add the basil, agave nectar, orange zest, vanilla extract, and peppercorns. Process on high until the chocolate is thoroughly melted and the mixture is smooth. Strain through a fine-mesh sieve.

Divide among 4 small cups. Cover and refrigerate until set, about 3 hours.

Per serving: calories: 348, protein: 3 g, fat: 28 g, carbohydrate: 23 g, fiber: 2 g, sodium: 13 mg, omega-3 fatty acids: 0 g

MANGOES AND LYCHEES WITH MINT

Makes 4 servings   (See photo facing page 135.)

I first devised this dish as an accompaniment to a coconut Bavarian cream I was serving after an Asian meal—later realizing it was sublime on its own, as a kind of exotic fruit compote. Then, after re-creating it for this book, I decided to combine it with my brand-new Coconut-Banana Sorbet (page 167), coming full circle (sort of). Again, it stands assertively on its own but exceeds triumphantly when served with the sorbet.

> 2 ripe mangoes
> 1 can lychees (see tip)
> 2 tablespoons brown sugar
> 2 tablespoons freshly squeezed lime juice
> 1 tablespoon grated fresh ginger
> 24 fresh mint leaves
> 4 scoops Coconut-Banana Sorbet (page 167; optional)

Peel the mangoes, and then cut them into cubes about 3/4 inch thick and put them in a bowl. Squeeze the juice from any pulp remaining on the pit into a separate small bowl and set aside.

Drain the lychees, reserving 1 tablespoon of the syrup.

Put the brown sugar and the tablespoon of lychee syrup in a heavy saucepan over high heat. Cook and stir for 2 to 3 minutes, until the sugar dissolves and the mixture caramelizes. Add the mangoes and stir gently a few seconds. Then add the lychees, reserved mango juice, lime juice, and ginger. Shake the pan as the mixture bubbles for about 1 minute. Remove from the heat and let cool slightly.

Gather the mint leaves into 2 or 3 stacks. Slice them crosswise into 1/8-inch shreds. Fluff slightly to separate them.

Divide the mango mixture among 4 bowls. Scatter one-quarter of the mint leaves on top of each serving. Serve at once, with a ball of Coconut-Banana Sorbet on top, if using.

Tip: Because all lychees come from Asia, the cans are often odd sizes. My favorite brand, for example, comes from Thailand and lists the net weight as 565 grams, with a drained weight of 230 grams. (Don't ask me how they can be that precise about the drained weight of fruit.) My suggestion is to just wing it with whatever size can of lychees you can find. The recipe will be virtually unaffected if you use slightly fewer lychees or a few more.

Per serving: calories: 183, protein: 2 g, fat: 0 g, carbohydrate: 43 g, fiber: 3 g, sodium: 35 mg, omega-3 fatty acids: 0 g

DRIED FRUIT COMPOTE

Makes 4 servings

This is mouth watering served warm on a cold winter night. If you've got a favorite vegan vanilla ice cream, this would be a good time to use it.

> 1 bottle sweet black muscat wine or other dessert wine
> 2 ripe, juicy tangerines
> ½ cup chopped dried apricots
> ½ cup dried wild blueberries
> ½ cup dried bing cherries (pitted, of course!)
> ½ cup dried cranberries
> ½ cup golden raisins
> ½ cup dried strawberries
> ¼ cup maple sugar
> 1 teaspoon freshly crushed cardamom seeds (without the pod shell)

Pour the wine into a saucepan and bring to a boil over high heat. Decrease the heat and simmer for about 10 minutes, until the volume of liquid is reduced by about half.

Using a vegetable peeler, pare the zest from the tangerines in long strips and set aside. Squeeze the juice into the saucepan with the wine. Add the apricots, blueberries, cherries, cranberries, raisins, strawberries, maple sugar, and cardamom. Simmer for about 10 minutes, stirring often.

Remove from the heat. Add the reserved zest strips, stirring them in well. Let stand for 10 minutes. Remove and discard the zest strips. Serve warm, in small bowls.

Per serving: calories: 397, protein: 3 g, fat: 1 g, carbohydrate: 65 g, fiber: 5 g, sodium: 18 mg, omega-3 fatty acids: 0 g

MINTED CHOCOLATE DREAM

Makes 4 servings

This ridiculously quick-and-easy yet elegant and delightful dessert is made without cream, although the result is very rich and creamy. Impossible, you say? Try it. You can get a small bottle of peppermint schnapps so you don't have to buy a full-size one (although it's great to have around for sipping in cold weather).

8 ounces vegan dark chocolate, chopped
1 cup boiling water
¼ cup flax oil
1 tablespoon peppermint schnapps (optional)
1 teaspoon peppermint extract
4 perfect fresh mint sprigs, for garnish

Melt the chocolate in a stainless steel bowl set over hot (but not boiling) water, stirring occasionally. Once it is melted, whisk in the boiling water, 1 tablespoon at a time. The chocolate will seize up at first, but keep whisking and adding the water until it becomes smooth and creamy. Whisk in the flax oil, peppermint schnapps, if using, and peppermint extract. Pour into 4 dessert goblets. Refrigerate until set, at least 2 hours.

Remove from the refrigerator about 20 minutes before serving. Garnish with the mint sprigs at the last moment. After your guests have begun their spasmodic utterances of blissful approval, you can go ahead and tell them what's in it. Show them the recipe if they don't believe you.

Per serving: calories: 520, protein: 2 g, fat: 42 g, carbohydrate: 32 g, fiber: 1 g, sodium: 0 mg, omega-3 fatty acids: 14.2 g

NUTTY CHOCOLATE BALLS

Makes about 24 balls

These are not to be confused with chocolate truffles (which, when properly prepared, are a near-religious experience), but they're quite scrumptious in their own right. I'm partial to hazelnuts, especially in combination with chocolate, but virtually any nut butter will produce delicious results. Use the best quality cocoa you can find—always!

½ cup Dutch-process cocoa powder
½ cup roasted hazelnut butter
½ cup agave nectar
1 cup chopped roasted hazelnuts or pecans

Combine the cocoa powder, hazelnut butter, and agave nectar in a small bowl and mix thoroughly. Cover and put in the freezer for 10 to 15 minutes—just long enough for it to firm up slightly.

Spread the hazelnuts on a small plate.

Remove the cocoa mixture from the freezer. Scoop out a small amount (about 2 teaspoons) of the mixture and form a ball. Roll the ball in the hazelnuts, pressing lightly to coat, and place on a clean plate. Repeat with the remaining cocoa mixture and nuts. Serve at once, or store in the refrigerator and eat at will.

Per ball: calories: 92, protein: 2 g, fat: 7 g, carbohydrate: 7 g, fiber: 2 g, sodium: 1 mg, omega-3 fatty acids: 0 g

SPICED PEAR SORBET

Makes about 1 quart

I once made the delightful mistake of buying a case of fully ripened, amazingly fragrant Bartlett pears (organic, of course), precipitating a wild spate of pear gorging. My family and I ate a bunch right off the core, then in fruit salad with peaches (another full case—I couldn't stop myself!) and raspberries, and then in oatmeal. Finally, when it looked like we wouldn't be able to eat them all before they went over the line, I made sorbet.

2½ pounds very ripe pears (Bartlett or d'Anjou work best)
½ cup agave nectar
3 tablespoons freshly squeezed lemon juice
1 teaspoon freshly grated and squeezed ginger juice (see tip)
1 pinch freshly crushed cardamom seeds
1 pinch freshly crushed cloves

Refrigerate the pears for 8 to 12 hours, if time permits. Peel and core the pears and put the flesh in a blender. Add the agave nectar, lemon juice, ginger juice, cardamom, and cloves. Process until smooth. Pour into an ice-cream maker and freeze according to the manufacturer's instructions.

Tip: The best results for juicing ginger are obtained by peeling a large rhizome and rubbing it across the grain on a Japanese ceramic ginger grater. Gather small amounts of the pulp as it accumulates on the grater and squeeze out the juice into a small cup or measuring spoon. You can do this either in a fine-mesh strainer or simply between your fingers. Once you have pressed out every last drop of juice, discard the pulp.

Per ½ cup serving: calories: 145, protein: 1 g, fat: 1 g, carbohydrate: 34 g, fiber: 4 g, sodium: 0 mg, omega-3 fatty acids: 0 g

SPICED PEARS IN WINE

Makes 6 servings

Poached pears make a very light dessert, with a hint of richness that satisfies the craving for something special after a great meal. I've served poached pears after Thanksgiving dinner, in place of all those heavy traditional pies, to rave reviews. Choose a fine dessert wine for this, but it needn't be too sweet since you'll be adding agave nectar. Look for Essencia, a California dessert wine made from orange muscat grapes. Failing that, any good Riesling will do. Bear in mind that there is no such thing as "cooking wine," so make sure it's drinking quality.

1 bottle dessert wine
½ cup water
½ cup agave nectar
3 bay leaves
7 whole cloves
¾ teaspoon whole black peppercorns
6 ripe pears, peeled, with stem left intact

Combine the wine, water, agave nectar, bay leaves, 1 of the cloves, and the peppercorns in a saucepan. Bring to a boil, decrease the heat, and simmer for 2 to 3 minutes. Stick the remaining 6 cloves into the 6 peeled pears (1 clove in each pear), just above where the fruit narrows at the stem end. Place the pears into the wine mixture. Return to a simmer and cook for 15 minutes. Remove from the heat. Let the pears cool in the syrup at room temperature for 8 to 12 hours.

To serve, remove the pears from the syrup and drain them well. Arrange them on a serving platter. Strain the syrup over the pears.

If you prefer to serve the pears warm, reheat them in the syrup gently, and then transfer the pears to a platter. Cook the syrup a little longer to reduce and thicken it (as it thins out a bit when heated). Strain the syrup over the pears.

Per serving: calories: 295, protein: 1 g, fat: 1 g, carbohydrate: 51 g, fiber: 4 g, sodium: 7 mg, omega-3 fatty acids: 0 g

COCONUT-BANANA SORBET

Makes about 1 quart

When I worked for millionaires, they would often notice a big bunch of bananas getting quite ripe and say, "You should make banana bread with these." I knew it was a lifetime of this sort of thrift mentality that eventually made them capable of hiring me, so I didn't bother telling them that it only takes about one and a half bananas to make a loaf of banana bread. This sorbet is a much better solution (and better *for* you). Very creamy. For an extra-sensual treat, add some small gobs of firm Minted Chocolate Dream (page 163) to the mixture after it comes out of the ice-cream maker, before it sets up in the freezer.

  1 can (13.5 to 14 ounces) coconut milk
  3 ripe bananas
  Zest and juice of 1 lime
  2 tablespoons agave nectar
  1 tablespoon premium dark rum

Combine all the ingredients in a blender. Process until smooth. Pour into a bowl, cover, and refrigerate until cold.

Pour into an ice-cream maker and freeze according to the manufacturer's instructions. If the sorbet is still too soft, scrape it into a chilled container and place it in the freezer to firm up before serving.

Per ½ cup serving: calories: 145, protein: 0 g, fat: 10 g, carbohydrate: 13 g, fiber: 1 g, sodium: 0 mg, omega-3 fatty acids: 0 g

ONLINE SHOPPING SOURCES

AMAZON

www.amazon.com

Having expanded from books to many other areas, Amazon offers an impressive array of culinary items, both equipment and ingredients. The only downside is that often these are sold through different vendors, so you might end up paying separate shipping costs for each item.

BIG TREE FARMS

www.bigtreebali.com

Despite high-end prices, Big Tree Farms stocks excellent palm sugar, finishing salt, and exotic pepper.

THE CULINARY DISTRICT

www.culinarydistrict.com

The Culinary District (formerly Surfas) carries a wide selection of gourmet ingredients, including chocolate, as well as kitchen equipment.

GOLD MINE NATURAL FOODS

www.goldminenaturalfoods.com

Gold Mine Natural Foods is a one-stop shopping source for macrobiotic ingredients, especially ones that may prove hard to find locally.

JB PRINCE

www.jbprince.com

JB Prince sells restaurant-quality kitchen tools and equipment.

MARKET HALL FOODS

www.markethallfoods.com

Market Hall Foods offers many specialty items that may not be readily available in stores near you, including whole-grain farro, farro pastas, and high-quality baking chocolate.

THE SPICE HOUSE

www.thespicehouse.com

The Spice House is an excellent source for high-quality herbs and spices at very reasonable prices.

THAI SUPERMARKET ONLINE

http://importfood.com

Thai Supermarket Online is a good source for Thai ingredients and cookware.

ABOUT THE AUTHOR

ALAN ROETTINGER has been a private chef to the stars for twenty-eight years, serving clients in the United States, Europe, and Australia. Raised in Mexico City, he acquired a taste for exotic food and culture early on—a passion for flavor and beauty that drives his culinary expression.

He has cooked in private homes, catered parties, and provided specialty desserts for a broad spectrum of high-profile clients, from entertainers to presidents. A world traveler, he absorbed elements from many cuisines to synthesize a unique, creative style of his own.

Throughout his years as a private chef, Alan developed a reputation for working within the limitations of restricted diets to create delicious food tailored to the specific tastes of each person. His first cookbook, *Omega-3 Cuisine*, showcases his ability to bring health and flavor together, offering a wide range of dishes that are simultaneously exotic and accessible to the home cook.

Visit www.alanroettinger.com.

INDEX

Recipes appear in *italicized* typeface.

BOOK PUBLISHING COMPANY
since 1974—books that educate, inspire, and empower

To find your favorite vegetarian and soyfood products online, visit:
www.healthy-eating.com

Also by Alan Roettinger

Omega 3 Cuisine
Recipes for Health and Pleasure
Alan Roettinger
978-0-92074-081-7
$19.95

Other great vegan cookbooks

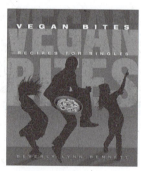

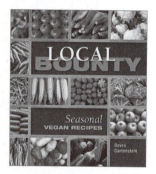

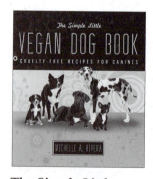

Vegan Bites
Recipes for Singles
Beverly Lynn Bennett
978-1-57067-221-7
$15.95

Local Bounty
Seasonal Vegan Recipes
Devra Gartenstein
978-1-57067-219-4
$17.95

**The Simple Little
Vegan Dog Book**
Cruelty-Free Recipes for Canines
Michelle Rivera
978-1-57067-243-9
$9.95

Purchase these health titles and cookbooks from your local bookstore
or natural food store, or you can buy them directly from:

Book Publishing Company • P.O. Box 99 • Summertown, TN 38483
1-800-695-2241

Please include $3.95 per book for shipping and handling.